Collins FLAGSHIP HISTORYMAKERS

GLADSTONE

GRAHAM GOODLAD

Dedication
To my mother, Mary Goodlad, and in memory of my father, David Astley Goodlad, 1929–2003.

Published by HarperCollins*Publishers* Ltd
77–85 Fulham Palace Road
London
W6 8JB

www.**Collins**Education.com
Online support for schools and colleges

First published 2004

ISBN 0 00 717320 2

British Library Cataloguing in Publication Data. A catalogue record for this book is available from the British Library.

Series commissioned by Graham Bradbury
Edited by Will Chuter
Design by Derek Lee
Cover design by Derek Lee
Map artwork by Richard Morris
Picture research by Noelle Moran
Production by Sarah Robinson
Printed and bound by Printing Express Ltd., Hong Kong

ACKNOWLEDGEMENTS

The Publishers would like to thank the following for permission to reproduce extracts from their books:

Longman for extracts from *Gladstone and the Irish Nation*, by J.L. Hammond (1938). Oxford University Press for extracts from *Liberal Politics in the Age of Gladstone and Rosebery*, by D.A. Hamer (1972). Routledge for extracts from *Gladstone and Kruger: Liberal government and colonial 'home rule' 1880–85*, by D.M. Schreuder (1969).

The Publishers would like to thank the following for permission to reproduce pictures on these pages (T=Top, B=Bottom, L=Left, R=Right):

Bettman/Corbis 7; Hulton-Deutsch Collection/Corbis 9L, 17, 26, 52; Corbis 39; Flintshire County Council 10; National Portrait Gallery 8, 9R, 24; Gwynedd County Council 21; Mary Evans Picture Library 33; Punch 34, 50.

Cover picture: Bettman/Corbis.

Contents

Why do historians differ?

THE purpose of the Flagship Historymakers series is to explore the main debates surrounding a number of key individuals in British, European and American History.

Each book begins with a chronology of the significant events in the life of the particular individual, and an outline of the person's career. The book then examines in greater detail three of the most important and controversial issues in the life of the individual – issues which continue to attract differing views from historians, and which feature prominently in examination syllabuses in A-level History and beyond.

Each of these issue sections provides students with an overview of the main arguments put forward by historians. By posing key questions, these sections aim to help students to think through the areas of debate and to form their own judgements on the evidence. It is important, therefore, for students to understand why historians differ in their views on past events and, in particular, on the role of individuals in past events.

The study of history is an ongoing debate about events in the past. Although factual evidence is the essential ingredient of history, it is the *interpretation* of factual evidence that forms the basis for historical debate. The study of how and why historians differ in their various interpretations is termed 'historiography'.

Historical debate can occur for a wide variety of reasons.

Insufficient evidence

In some cases there is insufficient evidence to provide a definitive conclusion. In attempting to 'fill the gaps' where factual evidence is unavailable, historians use their professional judgement to make 'informed comments' about the past.

New evidence

As new evidence comes to light, an historian today may have more information on which to base judgements than historians in the past. For instance, a major source of information about 19th-century political history is the Public Record Office (PRO) in Kew, London. Some of the information held at the PRO has remained confidential for up to 100 years. Therefore, it is only recently that historians have been able to analyse and assess this evidence.

A 'philosophy' of history?

Many historians have a specific view of history that will affect the way they make their historical judgements. For instance, Marxist historians – who take their view from the writings of Karl Marx, the founder of modern socialism – believe that society has always been made up of competing economic and social classes. They also place considerable importance on economic reasons behind human decision-making. Therefore, a Marxist historian looking at an historical issue may take a completely different viewpoint to a non-Marxist historian.

The role of the individual

Some historians have seen past history as being largely moulded by the acts of specific individuals. Gladstone, Disraeli and Lord Palmerston are seen as individuals whose personality and beliefs changed the course of 19th-century British history. Other historians have tended to play down the role of the individuals; instead, they highlight the importance of more general social, economic and political change. Rather than seeing Joseph Chamberlain as an individual who changed the course of political history, these historians tend to see him as representing the views of a broader group of individuals, such as the industrial middle class of late Victorian Britain.

Placing different emphasis on the same historical evidence

Even if historians do not possess different philosophies of history or place different emphasis on the role of the individual, it is still possible for them to disagree in one very important way. This is that they may place different emphases on aspects of the same factual evidence. As a result, History should be seen as a subject that encourages debate about the past, based on historical evidence.

Historians will always differ

Historical debate is, in its nature, continuous. What today may be an accepted view about a past event may well change in the future, as the debate continues.

Timeline: Gladstone's life

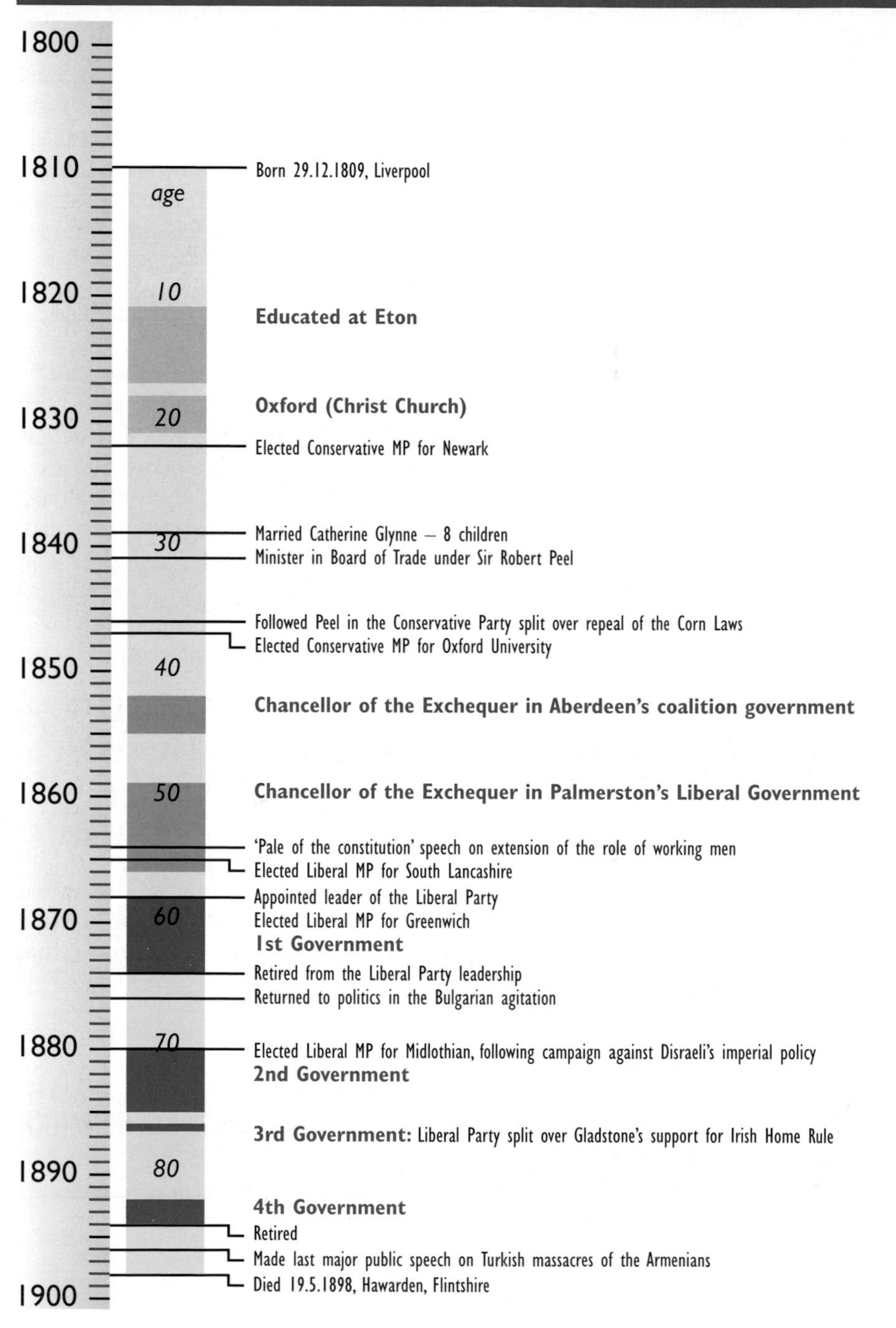

Gladstone in 1858, aged 49. This photograph conveys the seriousness and intensity of his public persona.

Gladstone: a brief biography

How did he make history?

WILLIAM EWART GLADSTONE (1809–98) came to embody the spirit of the Victorian age almost as completely as the Queen herself. This was partly the consequence of the extraordinary length of his political career: first elected to Parliament in 1832, he finally retired more than sixty years later. He remains a unique figure: the oldest person ever to take office as Prime Minister, he was also the only one to hold that post for four non-consecutive terms. Hardworking, serious-minded and a devout churchgoer, with a deep belief in individual liberty and moral responsibility, he exemplified what became known as 'Victorian values'. At the peak of his career as Liberal Party leader he polarised opinion, being idolised by his followers as the 'Grand Old Man', and attacked by the Conservatives as a threat to the British Empire and constitution.

Evangelical: a Protestant Christian with a strong belief in the importance of personal faith in God, and in the authority of the Bible.

High Anglican: a member of the Church of England who values the traditional authority of bishops and priests, and takes a Catholic view of the importance of the sacraments.

Free trade: the idea that goods should be exchanged between countries without payment of a tariff (tax or duty).

Liverpool, Eton, Oxford, Parliament

Gladstone was born into an upper-middle-class family. His father, a wealthy Liverpool merchant, ensured that he received the Eton and Oxford University education considered necessary for entry to the aristocratic political world. Brought up in an **evangelical** family background, as a young man he became a committed **High Anglican**. He entered politics, aged 22, as a Conservative whose main concern was the maintenance of the link between the State and the Church of England. His outlook became more practical as a result of his appointment, when he was 31, to ministerial office in the governments of **Sir Robert Peel**. Service at the Board of Trade and the Colonial Office enabled him to demonstrate a formidable grasp of administration. Yet he also remained consistent in his search for a moral purpose in politics. He advocated **free trade** on grounds of both economic benefit and ethical principle.

Sir Robert Peel (1788–1850)
Generally regarded as the founder of the Conservative Party, Peel was Prime Minister from 1834 to 1835 and again from 1841 to 1846. His decision to repeal the Corn Laws split the party and led to his downfall. This was because most Conservative MPs were landowners who believed that their interests had been betrayed. Gladstone was one of the small group of 'Peelites' who remained loyal to the ousted Prime Minister.

From Conservative to Liberal

Corn Laws: Between 1815 and 1846 the Corn Laws imposed tariffs on foreign grain imports in order to protect the economic position of British landowners and farmers.

Protectionism: the idea that all imported goods should be subject to tariffs, to protect production of domestic goods.

Italian nationalism: the movement to create a united Italy from the existing collection of separate states. British Liberals were particularly opposed to the Austrian Empire's domination of large parts of northern Italy prior to 1859.

Nonconformist: a member of one of the Protestant Churches other than the Church of England – for example Methodists, Baptists or Quakers.

In 1846, when Peel's decision to abolish the **Corn Laws** split the Conservative Party, Gladstone accompanied Peel and a small group of associates into the political wilderness. As time passed, he was unable to return to his old political home, which was increasingly dominated by Peel's great Conservative rival, **Benjamin Disraeli**. Although the Conservatives formally rejected **protectionism** in 1850, Gladstone found it hard to trust them on economic policy issues. From 1852 to 1855 he served as Chancellor of the Exchequer in Lord Aberdeen's coalition government, a position which enabled him to enact Peelite principles of balanced budgets, sound finance and tariff reduction. After the fall of the coalition government, Gladstone found more and more common ground with the Liberals. Although never personally close to **Lord Palmerston,** the Liberal leader, in 1859 Gladstone accepted his invitation to return to the Exchequer. Gladstone's belief in the need to control taxation and public expenditure, and his sympathy for the Liberal cause of **Italian nationalism,** brought him closer to the **Nonconformist** tradesmen and skilled workers who formed the core of the Liberal Party's grassroots. By the early 1860s he had become 'the People's William', a populist leader associated with support for the extension of voting rights to working men, religious liberty and other issues dear to rank-and-file Liberals.

1868: Liberal Party leader and then Prime Minister

The death of Palmerston and the retirement of his successor, Lord Russell, enabled Gladstone to assume leadership of the Liberal Party in 1868, aged 58. After winning the general election later that year he formed his first government as Prime Minister, often regarded as

Benjamin Disraeli (1804–81)
After helping to organise the backbench rebellion against Peel over the Corn Laws, Disraeli became leader of the Conservative Party in the House of Commons in 1849. A witty speaker and a clever parliamentary debater, his rivalry with Gladstone became legendary. Disraeli was Prime Minister from February to December 1868 and again from 1874 to 1880. He moved to the House of Lords in 1876, taking the title Earl of Beaconsfield.

Lord Palmerston (1784–1865)
Palmerston played an important role in the formation of the Liberal Party, and was Prime Minister from 1855 to 1858, and from 1859 to 1865. He was known for the forceful patriotism that he displayed in his conduct of foreign affairs, which earned him great popularity with the mid-Victorian public.

Disestablishment: the ending of the situation whereby the Church of Ireland was the officially recognised State Church for Ireland. Up to 1869 the Church received financial support from the Government.

his most successful. It carried out the **disestablishment** of the Church of Ireland and, through the 1870 Land Act, tried to address the problems of the Irish peasant farming class. It passed important reforms in the army, the civil service and the universities, gave legal recognition to trade unions and introduced the secret ballot for parliamentary elections. Yet reforms in other areas, notably in elementary education and licensing law, caused internal problems for the Liberal Party and contributed to its electoral defeat in February 1874.

Retirement, but not for long

In January 1875 Gladstone, now aged 65, retired from the party leadership. The leadership of the party was handed to Lord Hartington (the future Duke of Devonshire). However, Gladstone never resigned his seat in the House of Commons. He was unexpectedly drawn back into front-line politics the following year. The

Gladstone engaged in tree felling, one of his best-known pursuits, in 1877.

Understanding Gladstone

Gladstone was a complex man, made up of many characteristics:

- **A physically strong and active man**, whose hobbies included tree felling and extensive travel.
- **A widely read, scholarly man**, who combined a political career with the writing of serious books on classical and theological subjects.
- **A deeply religious member of the Church of England**, who believed that he was personally accountable to God for his actions.
- **A believer in the importance of individual charity**, who privately sought to rescue prostitutes from their life on the streets.
- **A skilled parliamentary debater.**
- **A passionate public speaker**, with an unrivalled ability to hold the attention of a large audience.
- **A great administrator**, with a mastery of detail, and enormous energy for work.
- **A practical politician**, who could change his position on public issues, whilst persuading himself and others that his actions were morally correct.
- **A consistent searcher for a moral purpose in politics**, even though he moved from the Conservative to the Liberal Party.
- **A controversial leader of the Liberal Party**, whose supporters saw him as a righteous crusader, whilst his opponents accused him of seeking to wreck the British constitution and the Empire.
- **Responsible for many radical changes**, such as the extension of the vote and the conversion of the Liberal Party to Irish Home Rule, yet always a social conservative who valued the land-owning aristocracy.
- **A meticulous diary-keeper.** His diaries have left us an invaluable historical source for his life and times.

'William Gladstone has not a single redeeming defect'
Benjamin Disraeli

occasion for his re-emergence was the development of a mass protest movement of unprecedented dimensions. The public outrage was over a moral and humanitarian issue – the massacre of Bulgarian Christians who were subjects of the Turkish Empire. Although Gladstone had not initiated the protest movement, he soon took it over. The 'Bulgarian agitation' spawned a broader assault on the foreign and imperial policies of the Disraeli government. Gladstone accused his rival not only of showing indifference to the sufferings of a vulnerable Christian people, but also of pursuing a costly and immoral policy of imperial aggression in the Afghan and Zulu Wars of 1879. In the run-up to the April 1880 general election Gladstone contested the Scottish parliamentary seat of Midlothian. In two highly publicised speaking tours, known as the Midlothian Campaigns, he mobilised public indignation against the Conservative administration, contributing powerfully to Disraeli's defeat and his own return to power, aged 70.

Prime Minister again: Gladstone's second government

Boer: a member of a race of Dutch settlers, also known as Afrikaners, who had established themselves in southern Africa.

Gladstone's 1880–5 government was marked by a series of crises and became known as 'the ministry of all the troubles'. There was a damaging conflict with the **Boer** settlers in South Africa, and a continuing problem of public order in Ireland. In 1882, disturbances in Egypt compelled Gladstone to authorise military action to protect the Suez Canal, a move which was at odds with his image as a man of peace. The occupation of Egypt drew him into further embarrassment when the officer charged with extricating imperial forces from neighbouring Sudan, General Gordon, was killed by nationalist rebels. This second Gladstone government had few positive achievements to its credit. The 1883 Corrupt and Illegal Practices Act took steps to regulate the conduct of parliamentary elections, whilst the 1884 Reform Act granted the vote to rural householders such as farm workers and miners. Gladstone's Commons defeat on the budget in June 1885 led to his government's replacement by a minority Conservative administration, which was only to last a few months.

Irish Home Rule and Gladstone's brief third government

Home Rule: a proposal, put forward by the Irish Nationalist Party, for Ireland to be granted its own parliament within the United Kingdom.

The final part of Gladstone's career was dominated by the issue of **Home Rule** for Ireland, which was demanded by a growing and increasingly effective Irish Nationalist Party. After the November

1885 general election, which produced an indecisive result, Gladstone took the political world by storm by letting it become known that he favoured Home Rule. He formed a third government in February 1886 and dedicated himself to bringing forward a Home Rule Bill. The proposal split the Liberal Party, causing a sizeable section of Gladstone's followers to create a separate grouping, the Liberal Unionists, who allied with the Conservatives in defence of the status quo in Ireland. Party division led to Gladstone's defeat in the Commons in June 1886, and he was ejected from office in the ensuing general election. His third government had lasted just six months.

Gladstone's fourth government

In August 1892, after six years in opposition, Gladstone, now 82, took office for the last time, with the support of the Irish Nationalist Party. His second Home Rule Bill passed the Commons but was rejected by the Conservative-dominated Lords in September 1893. The defeat of the Grand Old Man's last great political cause, together with failing health and eyesight, made his retirement almost inevitable. The actual occasion of Gladstone's March 1894 resignation was his opposition to his colleagues' proposals for increased naval spending. It was appropriate that Gladstone, the lifelong defender of controlled government expenditure, and apostle of a pacific external policy, should leave public life on such an issue.

Retirement at last

In retirement Gladstone continued to exert a powerful influence on his party. At the age of 86 he emerged to deliver one last great speech, calling for a response to the Turkish authorities' persecution of their Armenian subjects. When he died, in May 1898, Gladstone was accorded a state funeral in Westminster Abbey. It was an honour which reflected his standing as a national figure, placing him on a par with Sir Winston Churchill two generations later.

What was 'Gladstonian Liberalism'?

What were the constituent parts of Liberalism?

Was Gladstone an asset or a liability to the Liberal Party?

Framework of events

1859	Willis's Rooms Meeting – official formation of the parliamentary Liberal Party Gladstone appointed Chancellor of the Exchequer in Palmerston's government
1864	Gladstone's 'pale of the constitution' speech
1868	Formation of Gladstone's first government following election victory
1874	Electoral defeat of Gladstone; formation of Conservative government by Disraeli
1875	Gladstone retires from the Liberal Party leadership
1876	Publication of Gladstone's pamphlet *The Bulgarian Horrors and the Question of the East* marks his return to politics
1880	Gladstone forms his second government after successful Midlothian campaign against the Disraeli government
1885	Fall of Gladstone's second government; indecisive election result in November allows minority Conservative government to continue in office
1886	Gladstone forms his third government; Liberal Party splits on his Irish Home Rule proposals, which are defeated in the Commons (June) and in July general election
1891	Gladstone accepts the radical 'Newcastle Programme'
1892	Formation of Gladstone's fourth and last government
1894	Gladstone retires as Prime Minister

ALTHOUGH the Liberal Party was the dominant political force for a large part of the nineteenth century, historians have not found it easy to agree about its origins. The word 'Liberal' was in common usage from the 1830s, but politicians continued to use other labels, such as 'Whig' or 'Radical', for many years. June 1859 is often given as the date when the Liberal Party was formed as a parliamentary force. At that time several different groups of MPs, united by their opposition to Lord Derby's Conservative government and their sympathy for Italian unification, came together. Lord Palmerston, who took office after the Conservatives had been ejected from office, is often described as the leader of the first Liberal government. This did not mean that there was any attempt to create a national party, with a formal structure and mass membership, at that stage. Rather, historians have tended to see the early Liberal Party in terms of an informal but strong linkage between a parliamentary elite and a popular movement in the country, composed of a variety of different interests. We should also be wary of making a simple identification between Gladstone and the Liberal Party. Certainly he was the dominant figure in its development between the mid-1860s and his retirement in 1894. But he had not been involved in the formation of the party, and in several important respects his views remained distinct from those of a majority of Liberals.

What were the constituent parts of Liberalism?

The Liberal Party in Parliament represented the coming together of a number of traditions. Historians agree that the party was essentially a coalition, but there has been considerable debate regarding the relative weight and significance of the component parts. Perhaps the most controversial has been the Whig group.

The Whigs

The term 'Whig' was in widespread use in British politics from the late seventeenth century. Originally it denoted membership of an aristocratic faction that competed for high political office with its rivals, the Tories, who were the forerunners of the Conservative Party. Any discussion of the Whigs in the nineteenth century needs to begin with John Vincent's study, *The Formation of the British Liberal Party 1857–1868*, published in 1966. In this book Vincent adopted what now seems a restrictive definition of the Whigs, and consequently he dismissed them as numerically insignificant in the mid-Victorian Liberal Party. His definition of Whigs, however, included only those Liberal MPs who were members of a select group of aristocratic, land-owning families, such as the Russells or the Cavendishes. The involvement of these individuals in parliamentary life was determined by an inherited sense of duty and by a loose adherence to shared values. They were in politics because their ancestors had challenged the power of the Crown in the so-called **'Glorious Revolution' of 1688,** creating a political settlement in which the monarchy depended on a contract with Parliament, and civil and religious liberties were respected.

'Glorious Revolution' of 1688: the removal of King James II from the throne and his replacement by William of Orange, a Dutch Protestant prince, and his wife Mary. This was the work of a group of nobles who wanted the monarch to govern in accordance with the wishes of Parliament. Whigs looked back on this as a major turning point in the constitutional development of Britain.

More recently, historians have tended to adopt a broader definition of the Whigs, which has restored them to a more central position in the history of the nineteenth century Liberal Party. The most important contributions to the debate were made by Jonathan Parry in *Democracy and Religion: Gladstone and the Liberal Party 1867–1875* (1986) and by Terry Jenkins, author of *Gladstone, Whiggery and the Liberal Party, 1874–1886* (1988). These studies identified the Whigs with a tradition of leadership that extended beyond a handful of great landed families. Parry adopted the label 'Whig-Liberal' to denote an administrative elite of property-owning, Anglican politicians with a common belief in the cautious management of reform. Jenkins argued that the term 'Whig' became synonymous with the term 'moderate Liberal'. It included former Conservatives and 'Peelites' such as Lord Ripon, who did not belong to the charmed circle of historic Whig dynasties.

The Radicals

As with the Whigs, it has not been easy for historians to reach a consensus on the nature and strength of the 'Radical' section of the Liberal Party. This term has been used to describe a wide variety of MPs who wished to see far-reaching changes in one or more areas of politics and society. Relatively few were Nonconformist in religion; only 64 of the 382 Liberal MPs elected in 1868 could be categorised in this way. Radical MPs were usually drawn from the commercial and industrial world, and from the professions, and were opposed to the dominant place of the landowning classes in Victorian Britain.

Ideology: a body of ideas that influences political action.

It is hard to identify a common Radical **ideology.** These MPs shared certain general attitudes, such as a belief in liberty and justice, and a critical attitude towards the aristocratic establishment. They tended, however, to spread their energies across a number of different pressure groups or 'fads', such as Church disestablishment or the control of the alcoholic drink trade. It was common for an individual to believe that his particular enthusiasm was the key to wider social improvement. In addition there was considerable rivalry between different regional centres of Radicalism – Birmingham, Leeds and Manchester, for example.

Joseph Chamberlain (1836–1914)
Chamberlain made his reputation as a reforming Mayor of Birmingham before entering Parliament in 1876. He was a prominent Radical, who believed in the importance of a modern, professional party organisation. He also wanted the state to adopt a more active, interventionist role in social policy. He served as President of the Board of Trade from 1880 to 1885 and as President of the Local Government Board in 1886, but broke with Gladstone over Irish Home Rule and subsequently allied with the Conservatives. He served as Colonial Secretary from 1895 to 1903, eventually splitting the Conservative Party with his proposals for tariff reform.

National Liberal Federation: an organisation created in 1877 by Joseph Chamberlain to bring provincial Liberal Associations together and to push the Liberal Party in a more radical direction. Although based originally in Birmingham, it remained loyal to Gladstone in the 1886 Home Rule crisis and later relocated to London.

Joseph Chamberlain attempted to impose some order from 1877, with the creation of the **National Liberal Federation**, but Radicals in other areas were often suspicious of what they saw as a tool of one particular faction. In spite of Chamberlain's driving ambition and active promotion of reforming ideas, he never gained the degree of influence that he sought over the Liberal Party as a whole.

The Wider Liberal Party

Most Liberal MPs did not devote themselves to particular issues of reform but subscribed to a philosophy based upon a general belief in progress and improvement. At least until the mid-1880s, the typical MP was a land-owning country gentleman rather than an industrial manufacturer. In the 1874–80 Parliament, 46 per cent of Liberal members had aristocratic and land-owning connections, whilst businessmen accounted for less than 30 per cent of the total. Parliamentarians were, however, obliged to take account of wider Liberal opinion beyond Westminster. According to John Vincent's pioneering study, the party outside Parliament drew upon three main sources of support, which gathered strength in the mid-Victorian period. The first of these was religious Nonconformity, which expressed itself in a variety of pressure groups that were hostile to the privileged position of the State Church. The Liberation Society, for example, campaigned for the disestablishment of the Church of England, whilst the National Education League pressed for free, compulsory, **non-denominational education**. Secondly, from the 1860s skilled workers such as engineers were organising themselves in the so-called 'new model unions'. They sought to use the Liberal Party as a way of gaining legal recognition for their trade unions, in order to strengthen their capacity to bargain for improved wages and working conditions. Finally, popular Liberalism was underscored by the rise of provincial newspapers such as the *Leeds Mercury* and the

Non-denominational education: religious education that does not show bias in favour of a particular religious group, such as the Church of England, but which is based on general Bible teaching.

Manchester Guardian, whose growth was facilitated by the expansion of railways and Gladstone's removal of the taxes on paper in 1861.

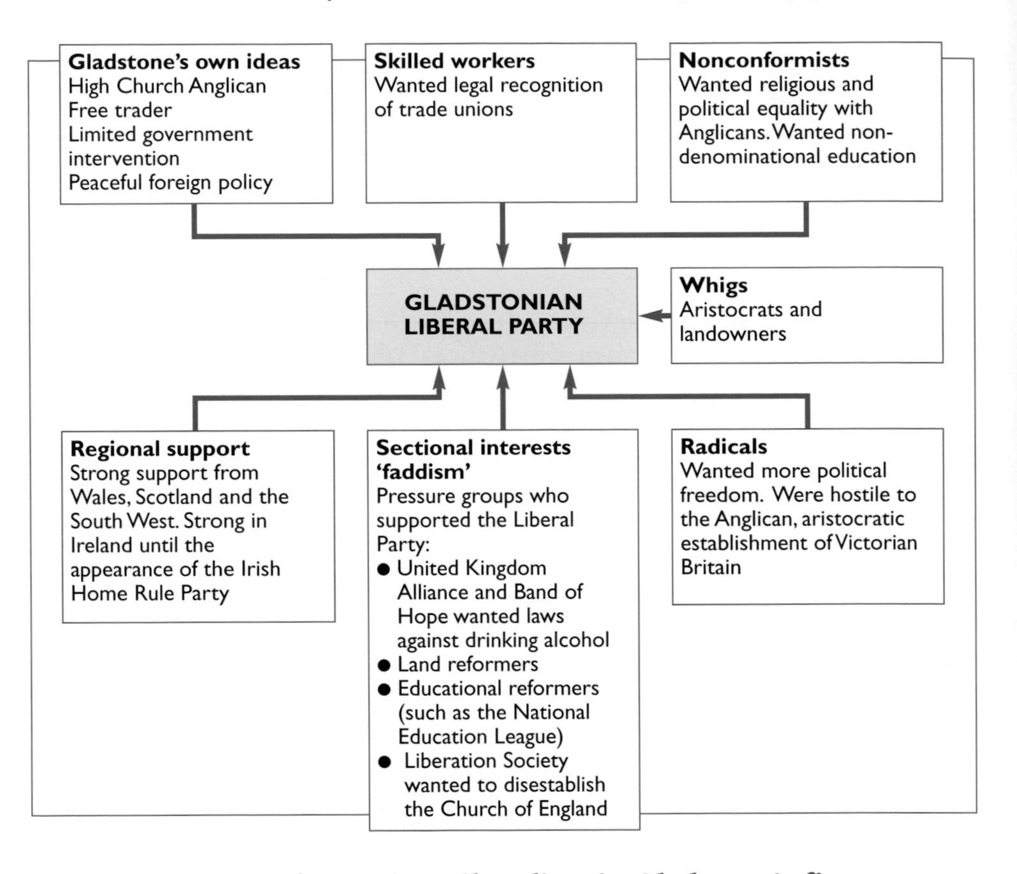

Implementing Liberalism in Gladstone's first government

Secret ballot: a reform introduced in 1872 in response to Radical Liberal pressure, which allowed people to vote by making a cross on a ballot paper in private. The aim was to end the practice of public voting, which left voters open to intimidation by landlords or employers.

Gladstone's 1868–74 government attempted to pass laws that appealed to the party's various constituent groups. The Prime Minister's main personal contribution was the passage of Irish Church disestablishment, the issue on which he had fought the 1868 general election, and which united Liberals of all shades of opinion. Thereafter he was generally content to allow individual government departments to enact legislation in their own areas. In many cases he took little interest in the actual content of policy, and he was privately unsympathetic to some issues. He supported the **secret ballot** with reluctance, as the price of retaining the co-operation of the Radical leader, John Bright. His main personal concerns, Irish legislation apart, were with the control of public expenditure and with measures to improve the efficiency of established institutions, such as the introduction of competitive entrance examinations in the civil service and the abolition of **purchase of commissions** in the Army.

The record of the 1868–74 government demonstrated just how difficult it was to frame practical legislation that kept all sections of the party happy. The Nonconformists who ran the National Education League, for example, were angered by the bias in favour of Church schools in the **Elementary Education Act (1870).** The 1872 Licensing Act, which restricted the opening hours of public houses, antagonised both the brewers and working-class drinkers, who resented moralistic state interference of this kind. On the other hand, it did not go far enough to satisfy the anti-drink fanatics of the United Kingdom Alliance, who campaigned for an outright policy of prohibition. Trade unionists won the legal status they desired in 1871, only to find their power to take strike action restricted by the government's Criminal Law Amendment Act.

Purchase of commissions: the practice whereby wealthy men were able to buy commissions as army officers. Its abolition in 1871 was intended to make the Army more efficient by linking promotion to merit.

Elementary Education Act (1870): an act which created the first state primary schools. In most areas the church remained the main provider of education, but where this was not possible, 'board schools', run by locally elected authorities, were to be created. The Act antagonised many Nonconformists because it permitted public funding of church schools.

Was there a common core of ideas and aims?

Given the diverse composition of the party, it is not very easy to identify a common set of ideas and aims that united all those who called themselves Liberals. John Vincent considered that Liberalism amounted to little more than a vague **humanitarianism,** and that 'coherent thought among leading Liberals was as rarefied as the atmosphere on the moon'. Gladstone was able to emerge in the 1860s as the hero of rank-and-file Liberals, whilst, at the same time, commanding the confidence of the party's parliamentary elite. This meant that his public image could be somewhat unclear. His radical-sounding public pronouncements, however, such as his 1864 **'pale of the constitution' speech**, allowed the party's Nonconformist and working-class supporters to create their own, idealised view of him.

Humanitarianism: a desire to do good to one's fellow human beings.

'Pale of the constitution' speech: in 1864, in a widely reported speech, Gladstone declared that 'every man who is not presumably incapacitated by some consideration of personal unfitness or of political danger, is morally entitled to come within the pale of the constitution'. The phrase was taken to imply support for a major extension of the vote to working men, and the qualifications which Gladstone included were not generally noted.

A related argument was developed by D.A. Hamer in his study of the party in the last quarter of the nineteenth century, *Liberal Politics in the Age of Gladstone and Rosebery* (1972). He too denied that the party had a common core of ideas and aims. Rather, it was a collection of sectional interest groups, each one intent on pursuing its own agenda at the expense of wider unity. Gladstone, according to Hamer, was uniquely able to impose order on the party by persuading these groups to subordinate their individual concerns to a single issue of overriding importance. According to this interpretation, Gladstone's support for Irish Home Rule in 1885–6 was a shrewd political move, even though it provoked a rebellion within the party and led to the loss of a general election. The important point was that the bulk of the party remained loyal to Gladstone, because they now had a clearly defined cause around which they could unite. In opposition after 1886, the leader was able to keep his followers focused by depicting the Irish issue as an 'obstruction' that must be cleared before the concerns of the party's various sections could be addressed. The analogy of an accident blocking a railway line was frequently used by Gladstone to make the point. In Hamer's words, 'in the absence of a Liberal creed, this single great question functioned as a substitute, conferring a provisional order on the miscellaneous and otherwise unco-ordinated interests in Liberal politics'.

These interpretations create a picture of a Liberal Party bound to its leader by strong but irrational ties. Vincent has argued elsewhere that rank-and-file Liberals' main gain from their association with the party was a sense of emotional uplift, derived from participation in crusades of right against wrong. Gladstone invested his great public campaigns with a sense of almost religious fervour. He claimed that his 1886 bid for Irish Home Rule put the sound common sense of ordinary people against the indifference of the privileged few on issues of justice: 'All the world over,' he declared, 'I will back the masses against the classes'.

Gladstone's appeal to 'the people'

The tendency in recent works by historians has been to take Liberalism more seriously and to see its supporters as being impressed by Gladstone's **charismatic leadership** but also capable of forming a considered judgement on quite complex issues. This is the interpretation put forward by the late H.C.G. Matthew (see **Landmark Study**, p24), editor of Gladstone's diaries. Matthew made the point that the majority of the electorate would have become familiar with the arguments put forward by Gladstone through the medium of the press, which reported the speeches of leading political figures in full. The speeches delivered in the 1879–80 Midlothian Campaigns required a considerable degree of sophistication on the part of their audience. According to Matthew, Gladstone's methods of communication with the public encouraged the growth of 'the concept of the active citizen', which was 'central to the **ethos** of Liberalism'.

A similar approach was taken by the historian Eugenio Biagini in

Charismatic leadership: a style of popular leadership based on the striking personal qualities of a commanding individual. The concept is associated with the German sociologist Max Weber (1864–1920).

Ethos: the distinctive character or moral outlook of a particular group.

Gladstone addressing an open-air meeting on Snowdon, Wales, 1892. Speeches like these were relayed to those who couldn't hear the speaker by individuals planted in the audience. Gladstone is on the ridge in the middle of the picture, behind a table.

Landmark Study The book that changed people's views

H.C.G. Matthew, *Gladstone 1809–1898* (Oxford University Press, 1997)

Professor Matthew edited the Gladstone Diaries, published in fourteen volumes between 1973 and 1994. Each volume began with a scholarly introduction, which provided important insights into the life and times of its subject. These introductions were later collected together and published in their own right as *Gladstone 1809–1898*. The publication of the diaries had a profound effect on the way that historians view Gladstone. They are a unique and detailed record of his activities and thoughts on a day-to-day basis. Matthew's introductions have also had an important influence on interpretations of Gladstone. They make clear the centrality of his religious beliefs to his political career, and the basic conservatism of many of his attitudes throughout his life. Another theme is Gladstone's use of public opinion. Matthew argues that, by communicating with a mass audience, Gladstone developed a new kind of leadership based upon the appeal of a charismatic individual. At the same time his approach encouraged voters to behave as active citizens, participating in rational debate about political issues.

his book, *Liberty, Retrenchment and Reform: Popular Liberalism in the Age of Gladstone, 1860–1880* (1992). Biagini placed Gladstonian Liberalism in an older tradition of popular radicalism, which had a powerful appeal to independent craftsmen, small employers and tradesmen, as well as to workers organised in trade unions. These groups saw themselves not as a particular class but as 'the people' – all those productive elements in society who had reason to oppose the unearned, inherited privileges of the aristocracy. Support for this kind of radicalism was strongest in the rural areas of southwest England and East Anglia, in the Midlands and the North East, and in Wales and Scotland. In these areas Nonconformity provided a strong ideological bond, bolstering a sturdy sense of community and of independence from aristocratic power and **patronage**.

Patronage: support and assistance given by a powerful person to those of lower social standing.

Biagini argues that Liberal themes of civil and religious equality, and of democratic reform, were widely understood and supported by these people. They also saw Gladstone's emphasis on retrenchment – the reduction of public expenditure – as being directly in the interests of ordinary people. They believed that 'unproductive' areas of national life, such as the armed forces and the diplomatic service, consumed unjustifiable amounts of public money. Liberals outside Parliament supported free trade as a way to lighten the tax burden for the mass of consumers, making the wealthy bear a proportionately larger share of the load. In this interpretation, the popular appeal of Gladstone was not only based upon the attraction of a charismatic leader, but was also inspired by the positive and rational aspects of his policies.

The religious dimension in Victorian politics

Secular: non-religious.

In a **secular** age like our own, it will never be entirely easy to understand the nature of Gladstone's appeal. As Jonathan Parry has reminded us, Victorian politics had a strong religious dimension, and religious issues, such as Church disestablishment and non-denominational education, enjoyed a remarkable prominence in the political debates of the time. Politicians were expected to promote religious ends in public life, and to safeguard social stability by ensuring that progress was made in the direction desired by God. My own investigation of the Home Rule crisis of 1885–6, published in my essay 'Gladstone and his rivals' (in *Currents of Radicalism,* edited by Eugenio Biagini and Alastair Reid, 1991) confirmed this view. At popular Liberal meetings during the 1886 general election campaign, speakers rarely mentioned the details of the Home Rule proposals, and concentrated on the moral righteousness of Gladstone and his cause. They considered that he was entitled to their support because, as a deeply religious person, he could be relied upon to recommend the morally correct course of political action. In this way he succeeded in acting as the uniquely qualified interpreter of Liberal principles.

Was Gladstone an asset or a liability to the Liberal Party?

Partly as a consequence of his Conservative-Peelite roots, and his High Anglican beliefs, Gladstone was never very representative of his party. As we have seen, his gifts as a popular leader made him the darling of the Liberal rank and file. He stood out for his ability to invest political issues with a moral imperative, and to convey his message to a mass audience using the media of the day. He was in step with Radical opinion on some issues, notably on Ireland, where he was prepared to restrict the property-owning rights of the landowners, and (from 1886) to grant self-government to the people. Yet, in spite of his criticism of the moral outlook of 'the upper ten thousand', he remained socially conservative. On one occasion he described himself in conversation as 'a firm believer in the aristocratic principle – the rule of the best ... an out-and-out inegalitarian'. Although he brought about the disestablishment of the Church of Ireland, and came to accept the same principle for Wales and Scotland, he continued to uphold the position of the State Church in England. He preferred the Church schools to the board schools created by his own government's Education Act, noting in 1877 that in matters of Church policy he was too much of a 'stiff denominationalist' to be in harmony with the 'average feeling of the party'. On the other hand, on civil questions he acknowledged that his 'opinions and leanings are too popular for the larger part of the aristocratic section of the party'.

According to D.A. Hamer, it was this refusal to be captured by any one element of the party that helped to give Gladstone his unique power over it. Radicals believed that they had sufficient common ground with him to stand some chance of achieving at least part of their programme. In any case his ability to harness public opinion made it unwise to contemplate breaking with him. At the other end of the political spectrum, at least until 1885–86, the Whigs saw him as a restraining force, whose leadership offered the best hope of averting a Radical takeover of the party. Indeed, Richard Shannon, author of the specialist study *Gladstone and the Bulgarian Agitation 1876* (1963), argued that this episode meant 'the ruin of Radicalism'. By re-entering politics and seizing control of the anti-Turkish protest movement in 1876, Gladstone effectively took over the Radical section of the party, diverting it from the fulfilment of its own agenda.

Other historians have challenged this view of Gladstone as a masterly leader, keeping control by mediating between two opposing wings of the party. In his study of the period 1874–86, Terry Jenkins argues that the importance of the Radicals who followed Joseph Chamberlain has been exaggerated, and that the Whigs did not organise themselves as a faction within the party. He has common ground with Jonathan Parry, whose views have been most fully developed in his book, *The Rise and Fall of Liberal Government in Victorian Britain* (1993). Parry argues that Gladstone's style of leadership disrupted an established Whig-Liberal tradition of national government, based upon the rule of an enlightened, property-owning elite. These representatives of 'mainstream Liberalism', like **Lord Hartington,** offered rational, orderly administration based upon a readiness to undertake necessary reforms and a consensus about what constituted the national interest. Gladstone's apparently democratic style aroused fears that he was prepared to subordinate the principles of good government to the emotionalism of moral crusades. His campaign for Irish Home Rule brought the unease of Whig-Liberals to a head. To grant self-government because of Irish Nationalist pressure seemed like surrender to an unrepresentative, lawless minority, placing vital British interests in jeopardy. In domestic politics, they felt that Gladstone was encouraging the worst instincts of the mob,

Lord Hartington (1833–1908)
A leading Whig member of the 1868–74 and the 1880–5 governments, Hartington served as party leader in the House of Commons during Gladstone's temporary retirement from 1875–80. He refused to serve in the third Gladstone government because of his opposition to Irish Home Rule. He served as leader of the Liberal Unionists, moving to the Lords as Duke of Devonshire in 1891.

'Political trinity at loggerheads' – a cartoon illustrating Liberal divisions, from the Conservative journal, *St. Stephen's Review*, published at the time of the 1885 General Election. Gladstone scatters copies of the Liberal Party Manifesto, while Lord Hartington struggles to prevent Joseph Chamberlain from throwing traditional institutions overboard.

whereas it was the duty of statesmen to tame and discipline popular enthusiasms.

Newcastle Programme: a set of policies put forward at the Newcastle conference of the National Liberal Federation in October 1891. They included Welsh and Scottish Church disestablishment, votes for all men, taxation of land and the introduction of district and parish councils. Gladstone had little sympathy with many of these, but had to accept them in order to keep the party loyal to his Home Rule policy.

Letting the party break up

Parry acknowledges that Gladstone had good qualities as Liberal leader, but in the end his sense of mission and his faith in 'the people' had disastrous consequences for the party: 'Gladstone's behaviour in 1886 turned the Liberal Party from a great party of government into a gaggle of outsiders'. The defection of most of the Whig-Liberals in 1886 left the party dependent on a range of Radical pressure groups. In particular, it came to reflect the 'Celtic fringe' of Welsh and Scottish nationalist elements, whose agenda compromised the Liberals' historic claim to represent a coherent British identity. Gladstone's reluctant acceptance of the 1891 **Newcastle Programme,** and the commitment of his last government to the demands of a variety of sectional interest groups, signalled the triumph of a new, and narrower, brand of Liberal politics. In addition, the departure of many of the party's wealthiest supporters, who now became **Liberal Unionists,** weakened its organisation at local level and reduced its capacity to run parliamentary candidates.

Liberal Unionists: Liberals (mostly Whigs and moderates) who left the Liberal Party on account of their opposition to Irish Home Rule. They worked with the Conservatives, and a number of them accepted office in later Conservative-dominated governments.

Other historians have taken a more positive view of Gladstone's contribution to the Liberal Party after 1886. In his book *Gladstone and Radicalism: the reconstruction of Liberal policy in Britain 1885–94* (1975), Michael Barker argued that Gladstone became more sympathetic to left-wing issues in the final decade of his career. In particular, he came to identify the cause of Irish freedom with the rights of labour in general, claiming that the Conservatives' policy of **coercion** in Ireland was also a potential threat to working people in Britain. He was outspoken in his support for the London dockers in their great strike in 1889, portraying them as victims of an unjust establishment. A similar line was taken by the historian David Powell in an important article entitled 'The Liberal Ministries and Labour, 1892–1895', published in the *Historical Journal* in 1983. Powell demonstrated that in his last government, Gladstone cautiously accepted a more interventionist social policy in an effort to satisfy the demands of an increasingly assertive labour movement. The government passed legislation, for example, to limit the working hours of government employees and railwaymen. Gladstone also appointed the Foreign Secretary, **Lord Rosebery**, to seek a settlement of a miners' strike in 1893; this was the first time that a minister had mediated in a national industrial dispute.

Coercion: the taking of emergency powers by government, in order to deal with problems of public order.

On the other hand, both Barker and Powell acknowledge the limitations of Gladstone's support for labour causes. For example, Gladstone was hostile to the **death duties** introduced by the Chancellor of the Exchequer, Sir William Harcourt, in 1894, although he accepted graduated taxation of the income derived from ground rents. In Cabinet, Gladstone personally vetoed proposals for the payment of MPs, a long-standing demand of those who wanted to see more working men in Parliament. The suspicion lingers that Gladstone was simply adopting some pro-labour measures, as the

Death duties: under Harcourt's 1894 budget, landed estates were to be valued on their real capital value and taxed, following the owner's death, on a graduated scale. This was the forerunner of modern inheritance tax.

Lord Rosebery (1847–1929)
Rosebery was one of the small number of Whig aristocrats who stayed with Gladstone after the Home Rule split. He served as Foreign Secretary in 1886 and again from 1892 to 1894, before succeeding Gladstone as Prime Minister. His premiership lasted little more than a year. Rosebery was a 'Liberal imperialist' who was close to the Conservatives in his belief that governments should actively support the British Empire.

minimum price needed to secure Radical and working-class support for his Home Rule crusade. To the end of his life he continued to voice mistrust of what he called 'constructionism', by which he meant a policy of state-sponsored social reform. It would be hard, therefore, to claim that the Grand Old Man was a forerunner of the **New Liberalism** of the Edwardian period.

New Liberalism: the thinking of many influential Liberals in the early 1900s, who wanted to see the state adopt a more positive role in tackling social problems. These ideas found practical expression in the reforms of the 1905–15 Liberal governments – for example the introduction of old-age pensions and National Insurance.

Leader of the working classes

One of the most positive judgements on Gladstone's later career has come from Eugenio Biagini, who argues in *Liberty, Retrenchment and Reform* that 'to the very end of his life he remained the unparalleled leader of the British working classes'. Biagini sees Gladstone's charismatic leadership as playing a crucial role in equipping Victorian Liberalism for the pressures of an increasingly democratic society. In his short study, *Gladstone* (2000), he challenged Jenkins and Parry with the argument that, by 1885, the Whigs were moving towards an inflexible conservatism and were therefore unsuited to leadership of a dynamic radical party. By contrast, Gladstone showed himself able to maintain the support of progressive opinion to the end of his active life. Biagini shows how Home Rule struck a chord with the **Lib-Lab MPs,** who had been sympathetic to the Irish cause since at least the mid-1870s. Home Rule was especially resonant for Welsh and Scottish Liberals, whose own experience of landlord domination stimulated nationalist feelings in their own parts of the United Kingdom. In Wales and Scotland, Gladstonian priorities gave new life to an older radicalism, delaying the rise of a specifically working-class Labour Party.

Lib-Lab MPs: Liberal MPs of working-class origin, sponsored by trade union funding, who were elected to Parliament in small numbers from the 1874 general election onwards. They generally accepted the policies of the official Liberal leadership and did not attempt to develop a specifically working-class viewpoint. An example was Henry Broadhurst, who became the first working-class minister (Under-Secretary at the Home Office) in 1886.

Gladstone's legacy

Gladstone had many failings as a party leader. It was not merely that he split his party and, by his dogged insistence on a continued commitment to Home Rule, saddled it with a policy that was unpopular with the electorate, at least in England. It was also that his style of leadership was **autocratic** and, with the passage of time, he was less inclined to consult his colleagues. He took little interest in the practicalities of formal party organisation. Yet, as H.C.G. Matthew argues, although the Gladstonian Liberal Party was transitory, it proved remarkably successful in integrating broad support, in terms of both social class and religion. Although Gladstone contributed little to the development of ideas on social welfare, in the Edwardian era the party united around issues that were closely associated with him. These were free trade, which Liberals of all

Autocratic: domineering or dictatorial

Tariff reform: a proposal associated with Joseph Chamberlain, for Britain and the empire countries to form a single economic bloc, by imposing tariffs on imports from non-empire countries. The policy was a direct challenge to free trade ideas and, by dividing the Conservative Party, it helped to lose them the 1906 general election.

shades of opinion were able to support after the Conservatives turned to **tariff reform**, and constitutional issues, in the form of a battle to curb the powers of the House of Lords. Gladstone's legacy to his party was not completely negative.

This September 1891 cartoon from *St Stephen's Review* unkindly suggests that Gladstone subsituted the force of his own rhetoric for concrete policy proposals.

What was 'Gladstonian Liberalism'?

1. Read the following extract and answer the question.

   'For Gladstone came to believe that one of the best ways of establishing order in Liberal politics was to attach Liberals to some great cause that would so impress them with its importance that they would voluntarily subordinate to it their special, divisive interests ...'

   (Adapted from D.A. Hamer, *Liberal Politics in the Age of Gladstone and Rosebery*, Oxford University Press, 1972, pp 63–4.)

   'Gladstone's greatest challenge as Liberal leader was to try to keep the Liberal Party together.' Using information in the extract above, and from the rest of this book, explain why this was such an important issue for Gladstone from 1868.

2. What do you regard as Gladstone's greatest success as Liberal leader from 1868 to 1894?

Was Gladstone a reluctant imperialist?

Did he neglect the Empire?

Did he have a coherent approach to foreign affairs?

Framework of events

1870	Russia rejects the Black Sea clauses of the 1856 Treaty of Paris
1870–1	The Franco-Prussian War
1872	The *Alabama* claims are settled by an international court
1873	Gladstone's government sends military expedition to the Gold Coast
1876	Gladstone leads the 'Bulgarian agitation'
1880	Gladstone returns to power after the Midlothian campaigns
	British troops withdrawn from Afghanistan
1880–1	First Anglo-Boer War in South Africa
1882	Bombardment of Alexandria and occupation of Egypt
1885	Murder of General Gordon at Khartoum
	Penjdeh incident with Russia over Afghanistan
1886	Upper Burma becomes part of the British Indian Empire
1894	Uganda becomes part of the Empire

Afghan War: a conflict caused in 1878–9 by the belief that Afghanistan must be occupied by British forces in order to make it secure against a possible Russian invasion. This was the initiative of Lord Lytton, Viceroy of India (with which Afghanistan shared a border). The Disraeli government was not directly responsible, but its image was damaged by the ensuing war.

THE phrase 'reluctant imperialist' comes from the title of a study by the historian C.J. Lowe, *The Reluctant Imperialists: British Foreign Policy 1878–1902* (1967). Although Lowe was seeking to analyse the actions of British policy makers in general, the phrase is particularly appropriate as a description of Gladstone. It indicates one of the central contradictions of his career. Gladstone publicly argued that the expansion of the Empire was not in Britain's real interests. He regarded overseas military adventures as expensive and dangerous. His outspoken condemnation of the **Afghan War** and the

The mid-Victorian Empire

By the 1860s, Britain stood at the centre of a worldwide empire. As well as Canada, Australia and New Zealand, it included territories in the West Indies and on the western and southern coasts of Africa. In the Far East, Britain controlled Hong Kong, Singapore and parts of the modern-day state of Malaysia. But the most important part was the British Indian Empire, which comprised the modern-day states of India, Pakistan, Bangladesh, Sri Lanka and parts of Myanmar.

Commercial and strategic value

The Empire had not developed according to a coherent overall plan. Some lands had been acquired for commercial reasons, others for their strategic importance to Britain. In particular, land had been acquired to ensure that the Royal Navy dominated the seas and oceans. The Cape of Good Hope (South Africa) and Malta were two examples.

Some territories were directly ruled by British officials and controlled from London by the Colonial Office. Other colonies of white settlement, such as those in Canada and Australasia, were increasingly granted their own self-governing institutions in the mid-Victorian period. From 1867, Canada had its own elected parliament, though Britain still controlled foreign policy and defence.

India

India was 'the jewel in the crown' of the British Empire. Until the 1857 Indian Mutiny (a major native rebellion), most of the country was run by a British-backed trading organisation, the East India Company. In 1858 the East India Company lost control and was replaced by direct British rule. Indian affairs were handled by the India Office in London, with a Secretary of State for India in the British Cabinet. The Viceroy, a representative of the Crown, ruled India from Calcutta. Some parts of India continued to be administered by native princes, who kept their privileges by means of treaties signed with their British overlords.

Formal empire and informal empire

In addition to the formal Empire, ruled by Britain, there were a number of areas which were subject to informal control, based on Britain's commercial supremacy. These included Uruguay and parts of the Chinese coast such as Shanghai. Supported by British naval power, these territories accepted Britain as the predominant power without a need for direct rule.

The Empire underwent its most significant period of expansion from 1880 to 1914. Britain took part in the so-called 'scramble for Africa', and extended its authority in the Pacific, Malaya and Burma (Myanmar).

Zulu War, for which he held the Disraeli government responsible, helped pave the way for his return to office in 1880. Yet there was a difference between what he said in the election campaign and the actual record of the second Gladstone government. Although he withdrew British forces from Afghanistan on taking office, his government closed with a confrontation with Russia in Central Asia. In South Africa he reached a peace agreement with the Boers in 1881, but only after going to war with them. More controversially, in 1882, his government invaded Egypt, leading to an occupation which did not end until the evacuation of the **Suez Canal** zone in 1954. It is hardly surprising that Gladstone's imperial policies have attracted considerable attention from historians.

Zulu War: a conflict between British forces and the Zulus, a black warrior race in southern Africa, in 1879. There are similarities with the Afghan War in that the lead was taken by the British government's representative in the region, Sir Bartle Frere, who believed that the Zulus were a threat to his country's power. He launched military action without specific authorisation from the Disraeli government.

Suez Canal: this waterway, linking the Mediterranean Sea with the Red Sea, was built by France in 1869. It was important, commercially and strategically, because it significantly reduced the journey time between Europe and India. Previously all ships had to travel around the southern tip of Africa (the Cape of Good Hope) to reach the East.

Did Gladstone neglect the Empire?

On several occasions during his career, Gladstone's political enemies accused him of neglecting the British Empire or even of seeking to dismantle it. In Disraeli's 1872 Crystal Palace speech, for example, he asserted that 'there has been no effort so continuous, so subtle, supported by so much energy ... as the attempts of Liberalism to effect the disintegration of the Empire of England'. Such allegations need to be viewed in the light of the Conservatives' wish to damage their Liberal opponents in the eyes of patriotic public opinion. The historian C.C. Eldridge offered a detailed assessment of the policies of the first Gladstone government in his book, *England's Mission: the imperial idea in the age of Gladstone and Disraeli 1868–1880* (1973). He showed how Gladstone's withdrawal of troops from New Zealand and Canada in 1869–70, which gave the Conservatives useful political ammunition, was in fact consistent with the policies of earlier governments. The purpose was not to weaken ties with Empire countries, but to make self-governing colonies responsible for their own defence as part of a cost-cutting review of Britain's overseas military commitments.

Gold Coast: a territory (now Ghana) in West Africa, in which Britain had had trading interests since the seventeenth century. British representatives had good relations with the coastal Fante people, which brought them into conflict with the Ashanti tribe, who lived inland.

Another aspect of Empire policy was explored by W.D. McIntyre in *The Imperial Frontier in the Tropics 1865–1875* (1967). He examined the reasons for British imperial expansion in the **Gold Coast** and parts of the Pacific, particularly Fiji and Malaya. Although the Conservatives took the credit for the extension of British authority after they returned to power in 1874, the key decisions in these areas had been taken by the first Gladstone government. Gladstone himself was personally unenthusiastic about the acquisition of new overseas commitments, and the initiative was taken by other ministers and officials, who for the most part were responding to developments on the ground. In the case of the Gold Coast, the Colonial Secretary, Lord Kimberley, and the War Secretary, Edward Cardwell, organised a military expedition with almost no consultation of the Prime Minister and their other colleagues. Gladstone was, however, reconciled to the extension of British influence after the expedition secured a rapid and inexpensive success.

Gladstone's reservations about the cost of a 'forward' policy distinguished him from Disraeli. Disraeli adopted the imperial cause partly because of its domestic appeal. As the historian Muriel Chamberlain stated in *'Pax Britannica'? British foreign policy 1789–1914* (1988), this did not mean that Gladstone was hostile to the Empire itself. On the contrary, he saw its maintenance as a duty and a responsibility. His objection was to its further expansion.

In *Gladstone 1809–1898* (1997), H.C.G. Matthew endorses this interpretation, arguing that he was 'not anti-Empire, but … anti-imperialist'. It was a position which meant that, by the 1880s, Gladstone was out of step with the course of events. By that stage the potential for conflict on the borders of the Empire had grown significantly. European powers were competing with each other for overseas territory and, as the **General Gordon** affair showed, domestic opinion in Britain was unforgiving towards leaders who seemed to be half-hearted about the defence of the Empire. Gladstone's response was further complicated, according to Matthew, by a tension between two sides of his personality. On the one hand was his support for free trade and economy, which moved him towards a cautious reduction of direct British control. On the other hand, wrote Matthew, his 'executive itch, his sense of the immediate, of what seemed to be "practical", encouraged imperial action, eventually as bold as that of any other Victorian'.

The General Gordon Affair

General Charles Gordon (1833–85) was a British military hero sent by Gladstone to manage the withdrawal of British-controlled forces from the Sudan. He chose to remain at the capital, Khartoum, to confront a movement led by the Mahdi, an Islamic nationalist figure, and, after a nine-month siege, was killed in 1885. Gladstone's slowness to send a relief expedition to rescue Gordon made him extremely unpopular in Britain. This cartoon criticises Gladstone's conduct of the affair by portraying him as a camel. Camels were a common (and very slow) means of transport in the Sudan at that time.

Afghanistan: maintaining a successful buffer state

The conflict within Gladstone's personality was to be borne out by the record of his second government. Its imperial policies were largely conditioned by the legacy of the 1874–80 Disraeli government. In Afghanistan and South Africa, Gladstone's Liberal ideals seemed to suggest a retreat from the entanglements entered into by the outgoing Conservative ministry. Most historians have considered that Gladstone made the best of a difficult situation in Afghanistan, at least. He withdrew British troops, whilst successfully keeping Afghanistan as an independent **buffer state** against further Russian expansion towards Britain's Indian empire. This return to the pre-Disraelian strategy of 'masterly inactivity', behind defensible frontiers, contrasted with the more aggressive 'forward' policy pursued under the Conservatives. In the **Penjdeh incident** of 1885, Gladstone took an unexpectedly tough line, reinforcing Britain's military strength in order to deter a Russian advance into Afghanistan. Although his government fell from office in June 1885,

Buffer state: a country which acts as a barrier between two rival states.

Penjdeh incident: in March 1885 Russian troops threatened the settlement of Penjdeh, just over the Afghan border. Gladstone mobilised troops, in order to deter a possible later Russian challenge to Britain's control of India, before a negotiated settlement was reached.

before the crisis was resolved, it was settled by the incoming Conservative government along lines laid down by Gladstone. Penjdeh itself was given back to Afghanistan by the Russians. In *The Mid-Victorian Generation 1846–1886* (1998), K.T. Hoppen sums up the view of most historians, that it was 'a rare and almost total Liberal success'. The land approaches to India had been secured without a costly military commitment, in a way which avoided domestic political controversy.

A *Punch* cartoon, from the time of the Penjdeh crisis, commenting on Gladstone's movement from confrontation to negotiation with Russia.

OUR PROTEAN PREMIER!

(As "The Angel of Peace," in his Unrivalled Variety-and-Quick-Change Entertainment.)

South Africa: control by conciliation

Gladstone's handling of the Disraelian inheritance in South Africa was more controversial. The Boer Transvaal Republic had accepted **annexation** in 1877, as the price of British protection against the Zulus. Once the Zulus had been crushed, and a new government had taken office in Britain, the Boers expected the speedy restoration of their right to self-determination. When Gladstone did not at once concede this, they invaded the neighbouring British colony of Natal and inflicted a military defeat at the Battle of Majuba Hill in February 1881. Resisting the temptation to seek revenge, Gladstone pursued a policy of conciliation. The Pretoria Convention of August 1881 gave the Boers their essential demands, with independence for the Transvaal, subject to British **suzerainty**. This was confirmed by the London Convention of 1884.

Annexation: the take-over of one country by another.

Suzerainty: an arrangement whereby a country has control over its own internal affairs but its foreign relationships are supervised by another state.

Contemporaries criticised Gladstone for making concessions from a position of weakness. This view tended to overshadow the degree of continuity with the approach taken by Gladstone's Conservative predecessors. As the historian C.F. Goodfellow showed in his study *Great Britain and South African Confederation 1871–1881* (1966), Gladstone's aim was to maintain Britain's influence in the region, whilst avoiding direct administrative responsibility. In order to achieve this, initially he sought to revive the concept of **confederation**, towards which the Conservatives had already been working. The Boer rebellion of 1880–1 made this an impossibility. Nonetheless, as D.M. Schreuder argued in *Gladstone and Kruger: Liberal government and colonial 'home rule', 1880–85* (1969), Gladstone tried to maintain British influence by other means. The aim of the Pretoria Convention of 1881 was to combine local self-government with a loose imperial overlordship, as the only practicable alternative to a costly and unwinnable war against the Boers. According to Schreuder, Gladstone feared that the Transvaal might link up with the Dutch-speaking population in the British territory of Cape Colony. His policy may have been based on an exaggerated estimate of Boer solidarity, but it is understandable as an attempt to exercise influence at a distance, with minimal cost.

Confederation: an association of states which retain their individual power of self-government.

Egypt: what made Gladstone take military action?

Gladstone's policy towards Egypt and the Suez Canal has been a subject of even greater historical debate. In opposition, he had denounced Disraeli for purchasing the **Khedive's shares in the Suez Canal**. Writing in 1877, he criticised the Conservative government's

Khedive's shares in the Suez Canal: Egypt was part of the Turkish Empire but was run by an Egyptian governor, the Khedive Ismail. By 1875 he was almost bankrupt and was therefore ready to sell his investment in the Suez Canal to Britain.

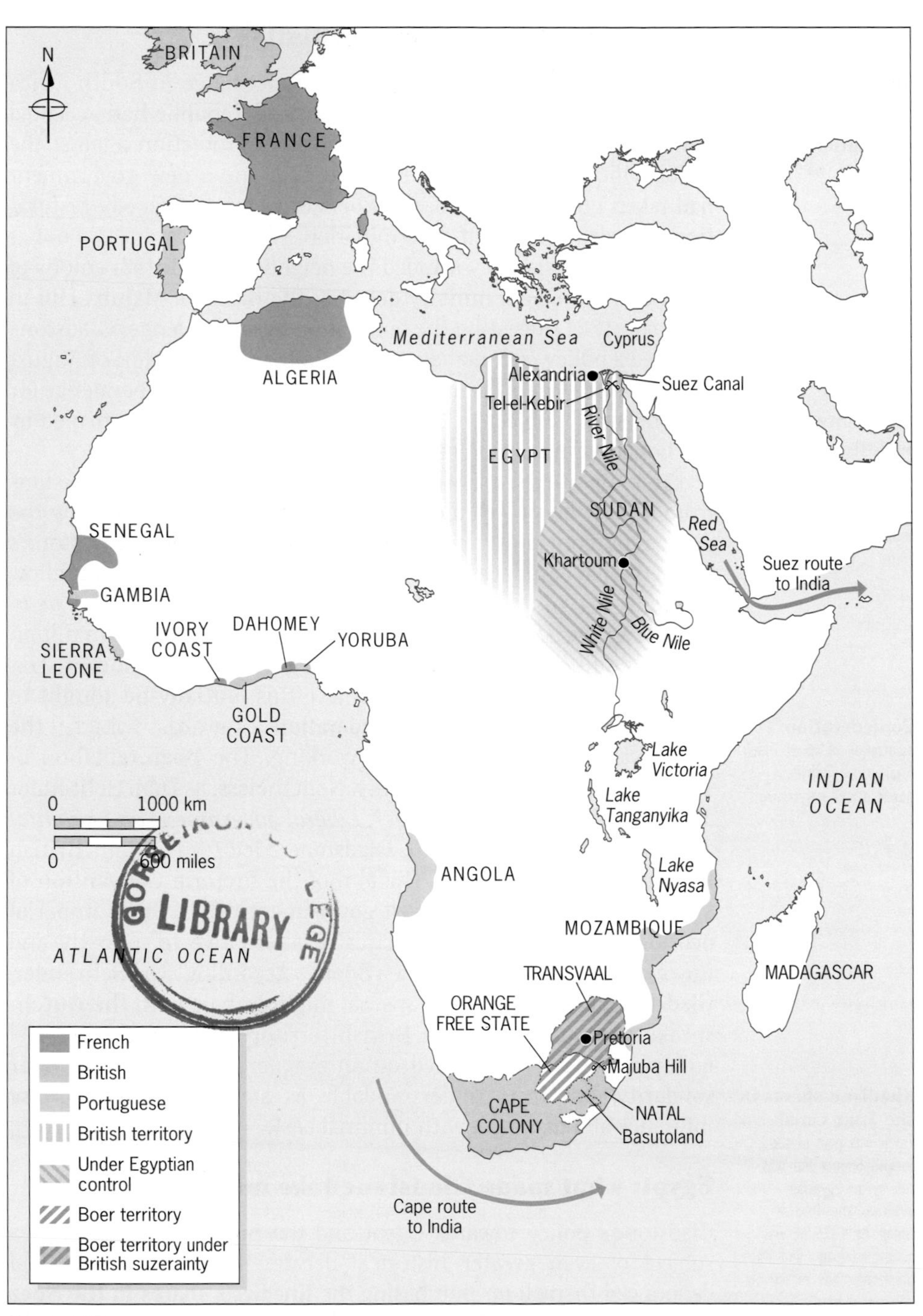

Africa in 1882.

obsession with defence of the route to India, and warned against involvement in Egypt, which would create 'the almost certain egg of a North African Empire'. Yet in July 1882 Gladstone took military action against an Egyptian nationalist movement, bombarding Alexandria and sending in troops to occupy the country. He rejoiced at the defeat of the Egyptian leader, Colonel Arabi Pasha, at the Battle of Tel-el-Kebir, in September 1882. Not only did this seem a flagrant violation of Gladstone's principles, it also ironically fulfilled the warning that he had issued five years earlier. Britain was to expand its territory in eastern Africa in the late nineteenth century as a consequence of its involvement in Egypt. Why, then, did Gladstone take action with such far-reaching consequences?

Strategic value of the Suez canal

Dual Control: in order to save Egypt from bankruptcy, British and French officials jointly managed the country's finances. Together with the removal of Khedive Ismail, who was replaced by his son Tewfik in 1879, it created an impression of intolerable interference by European powers in Egypt's affairs.

The starting point for modern historical debate on this issue was Ronald Robinson and Jack Gallagher's 1961 book, *Africa and the Victorians: the official mind of imperialism* (see **Landmark study**, below). They traced the way in which, from 1876, European intervention in the form of the **Dual Control** triggered a nationalist revolt which threatened the security of the Suez Canal. As law and order began to break down in Egypt in 1881–2, Gladstone hoped either for Turkish intervention or for joint European action in the region. It was only when France, paralysed by an internal political crisis, declined to act that Gladstone reluctantly approved unilateral British intervention. For Robinson and Gallagher, the crucial issue

Landmark Study **The book that changed people's views**

R. Robinson and J. Gallagher, *Africa and the Victorians: the official mind of imperialism*
(Macmillan, 1961)

Until the publication of *Africa and the Victorians,* most historians had argued that the main driving force behind the expansion of empire was the promotion of trade and investment. Robinson and Gallagher broke new ground by focusing on strategic rather than economic factors. They argued that Britain extended its territory in Africa in response to threats to the security of its communications with India and the East. Egypt, and in particular the Suez Canal, had become a vital line of communication to Britain's Indian Empire. The need to secure the Canal led to the need to keep control of Egypt. This, in turn, led to the need to control the River Nile. This forced Britain to take control of the Sudan and Uganda.

Gladstone's occupation of Egypt was particularly important because the anxieties it created among other European powers led to the so-called 'scramble for Africa' – a competition to gain new colonies that rapidly led to the carving up of Africa between them. Similarly, South Africa and the Cape of Good Hope were strategically important because they controlled the sea route between the Atlantic and Indian Oceans. To control the Cape, the British were forced to extend their control inland. Consequently, by 1902 Britain controlled the whole of southern Africa.

Robinson and Gallagher's arguments have not been universally accepted; in particular, some historians have suggested that the 'scramble' was under way before the invasion of Egypt. Nonetheless, their work permanently changed views on the period and the reasons for the growth of the British Empire in Africa.

for the Liberal government – as it would have been for a British government of any party – was the need to protect the Suez Canal: 'the security of the routes to the East was the one interest with which British cabinets could not afford to gamble'. Gladstone certainly did not envisage a long-term British occupation of the country. He hoped for a speedy 'police action' to restore order, followed by a rapid evacuation of British forces.

Domestic political considerations also played a part. With Whigs like Lord Hartington pressing for an assertion of British power, and with simultaneous difficulties in Ireland, Gladstone had little choice if he wished to preserve the unity of his government. This point also featured in the analysis of C.J. Lowe in *The Reluctant Imperialists*. Lowe presented Gladstone as extremely unwilling to take independent action, and personally unconvinced by the arguments surrounding the security of the Canal. He was pushed into intervention by the threat of a Cabinet rebellion. This would have ended his chances of settling the Irish question, with which he was more concerned at the time.

Protecting Egypt's economy

A different interpretation was offered by two economic historians, P.J. Cain and A.G. Hopkins, in *British Imperialism: innovation and expansion 1688–1914* (1993). Their work focused on the concept of 'gentlemanly capitalism', the idea that key decisions were influenced by a powerful elite of British financial interests, centred in the City of London and closely linked to the land-owning classes who dominated Victorian government. They argued that the crucial issue was not the safety of the Suez Canal but the Egyptian nationalist movement's desire to gain control of the Egyptian budget. Gladstone's government was drawn into Egypt, not by strategic considerations, but by the fear that political anarchy would jeopardise the management of the country's debt. In order to maintain good financial order it was vital to ensure that the debts owed to European **bondholders** were regularly serviced. This argument reappeared in H.C.G. Matthew's *Gladstone 1809–1898*. Matthew noted that Gladstone himself was an Egyptian bondholder. He acquits his subject of the suggestion of any personal corruption or wrongdoing, but still notes that over one-third of his investments took the form of Egyptian tribute loan.

Bondholders: people to whom a government or a company has issued promises, to enable it to raise money by borrowing.

Eugenio Biagini has contributed to the debate on Egypt in an important article entitled '"Exporting Western and Beneficent Institutions": Gladstone and Empire, 1880–1885'. Biagini argues that Gladstone did not have an absolute commitment to self-government for peoples in all circumstances. Instead it was dependent on the establishment of financial soundness, according to Western Liberal expectations. In Gladstone's mind, the eventual concession of self-government was linked to the need for responsible financial management.

Was Gladstone ahead of his time?

In Egypt, as in other areas, Gladstone certainly acted as a 'reluctant imperialist'. It was a stance which increasingly differentiated him from many other senior Liberals. A number of his Cabinet colleagues had misgivings about his readiness to see Germany acquire African colonies during the final year of his 1880–85 ministry. Whereas he believed that this might promote a spirit of co-operation, more empire-minded men feared the rivalry of a new and increasingly powerful competitor. During his last government, 1893–4, he disapproved of the British annexation of Uganda, which was eventually carried on the initiative of the Foreign Secretary, Lord Rosebery. In his preference for an empire based on self-government and voluntary association, in many ways Gladstone anticipated the more distant future. It was his misfortune to govern in an era when the prevailing international conditions made the realisation of such a vision improbable.

Did Gladstone have a coherent approach to foreign affairs?

Gladstone has often been seen as an impractical idealist in foreign affairs. The rise of a united Germany from 1871, under the direction of **Otto von Bismarck,** and the start of competition between the great powers for territory in Africa, made the last quarter of the nineteenth century an unfavourable time for foreign policies based upon moral principles. Historians sympathetic to Gladstone have commended him for a noble attempt to set a higher standard of

Otto von Bismarck (1815–98)
Minister-President of Prussia from 1862–90, and Chancellor of Germany from 1871–90. He played a leading role in making Germany a strong, united nation, and dominated international relations through a series of agreements with the great powers. His philosophy was based upon the self-interested exercise of power, and he regarded Gladstone and Liberalism with contempt.

international morality, whilst others have regarded his approach as simply unrealistic and doomed to failure .

A classic positive interpretation of Gladstone's philosophy is to be found in the work of J.L. Hammond, who was writing in the first half of the twentieth century. Although his *Gladstone and the Irish Nation* (1938) is not primarily concerned with foreign affairs, it is important for its attempt to place the Liberal leader in a broader European context. Hammond argued that Gladstone had a long-standing and strongly-held sympathy with the struggles of small nations, such as Italy and Norway, to develop an independent, self-governing life. He attributed this sympathy to Gladstone's classical education and deep moral sense, which enabled him to rise above the narrow prejudices of many of his contemporaries: 'it was now a battle between men moving within the circle of an island mind and a man who lived in the wisdom of the ages'.

Gladstone was a hero to men like Hammond, whose own centre-left political sympathies in the 1930s inclined them to see international co-operation, in the form of the **League of Nations,** as the best defence against the aggressive designs of dictators like Mussolini and Hitler. A similar view was held by the historian Paul Knaplund, whose more detailed study of *Gladstone's Foreign Policy* appeared in 1935. He described his subject's guiding principles as faith 'in the perfectibility of man and his institutions, in the ultimate victory of right over might, in the healthy qualities of freedom'. Knaplund's study demonstrated how a combination of adverse foreign and domestic circumstances frustrated Gladstone in the fulfilment of his vision.

League of Nations: an international organisation created after the First World War to promote international peace and disarmament. It was the forerunner of today's United Nations.

Gladstone's principles

Two central themes can be identified in Gladstone's thinking on foreign affairs:

- The first was a belief in nationality – that a people united by a common culture and tradition should have the right to determine their own future.
- Secondly, he wanted to reactivate the idea of the Concert of Europe, or co-operation between the great powers. In the early nineteenth century the 'Concert' had been interpreted by the leading European states in a conservative sense. It implied action by the established powers, such as Austria, Prussia (later Germany) and Russia, to maintain a **balance of power** and to suppress movements for radical change. By contrast, Gladstone

Balance of power: the idea that no single state should be allowed by the others to dominate the continent of Europe.

wanted to see it used to promote **ethical** objectives in foreign affairs. He hoped that other leaders would support his wish to uphold **the rule of law** in the interests of justice between the nations. United action would carry much greater moral authority than unilateral moves by individual states, acting in their own selfish interest. As he wrote in 1878, he wanted to see 'the pursuit of objects which are European by means which are European, in concert with the mind of the rest of Europe and supported by its authority'.

Ethical: basing one's actions upon moral principles, rather than simply following a policy of self-interest.

Rule of law: the idea that relations between states are governed by certain rules of conduct.

Pacifist: holding to the belief that war is morally wrong.

***Alabama* claims**: the *Alabama* was a ship built in Britain, and used by the Southern side in the American Civil War (1861–5) to attack Northern shipping. After the war, the United States government demanded compensation from Britain for the damage that had been inflicted. The Conservatives attacked Gladstone's settlement of the dispute as an example of his weakness in standing up for British interests.

Arbitration: the submission of a dispute between two parties to the independent judgement of a neutral body.

Within the Liberal Party, Gladstone's views were different from those of the so-called Manchester School, associated with Radicals such as Richard Cobden (1819–65). This group of Liberal thinkers took its name from the city which traditionally was the centre of mid-Victorian economic growth based upon free trade. Cobden and his followers argued that free trade would promote international co-operation, and that there should be no need for states to maintain large military resources. They were largely **pacifist** in their attitudes, and believed that Britain should pursue a peaceful, non-interventionist overseas policy. Gladstone sympathised with the Cobdenites; for example, in 1872 he braved 'patriotic' domestic criticism to resolve the long-running ***Alabama* claims** issue by means of international **arbitration.** However, he rejected their argument that Britain should never resort to military action. In the last resort, in order to defend important principles, 'there are times when justice, when faith, when the welfare of mankind requires a man not to shrink from the responsibility of undertaking [wars]'.

Gladstone's first ministry 1868–74

Franco-Prussian War (1870–1): a conflict between France and Prussia, which was crucial to the unification of Germany under Prussian leadership. France suffered a heavy defeat and lost the border territory of Alsace-Lorraine to Germany at the end of the war.

Gladstone was certainly prepared to use moral and diplomatic pressure to resist threats to international law. For example, when the **Franco-Prussian War** broke out, his government secured undertakings from both sides to respect Belgium's neutral status. Indeed, in his desire to protest at Germany's take-over of Alsace-Lorraine, Gladstone wished to go further than his Cabinet colleagues, who successfully overruled him. On this issue he was at odds not only with Cobdenite Radicals but also with Whigs such as Lord Granville (Foreign Secretary 1870–4 and 1880–5), who preferred the more secretive practices of traditional diplomacy. Gladstone responded with an anonymous article (which was at once identified as his work) in which he expressed confidence in the acceptance of 'the general judgement of civilised mankind' and the concept of 'Public Right as the growing idea of European policy'.

An important analysis of Gladstone's policies is to be found in Muriel Chamberlain's study, *'Pax Britannica'? British Foreign Policy 1789–1914.* Chamberlain sees Gladstone as a realist in his moderate approach to the *Alabama* claims, the Franco-Prussian War and Russia's breach of the **Black Sea clauses.** The deciding factor, she argues, was the limited size of Britain's military forces, which restricted the possibilities of effective intervention.

Black Sea clauses: the 1856 Treaty of Paris, which ended the Crimean War, prohibited Russia from maintaining a battle fleet in the Black Sea. The purpose of this was to prevent Russia from challenging Britain's naval dominance in the Mediterranean. In 1870, during the Franco-Prussian War, Russia rejected the clauses. Gladstone was unable to prevent this, but registered international disapproval of unilateral action by summoning a conference in London.

A more critical view is to be found in the work of another historian, Kenneth Bourne's *The Foreign Policy of Victorian England 1830–1902* (1970). He argues that Gladstone was able to summon a conference on the Black Sea clauses only because Bismarck put pressure on Russia to accept. Bismarck was involved in the Franco-Prussian War at the time and feared British intervention. After the war, Germany, Russia and Austria soon reached agreement between themselves, leaving 'neutral and liberal England in virtual isolation'. Undoubtedly the defeat of France and the creation of a united Germany profoundly altered the European balance of power, a reality which was grasped more clearly by Gladstone's rival, Disraeli. Yet, with an army ill-equipped to threaten much larger continental forces, it is hard to see how any British government could have responded more decisively at the time.

The Bulgarian agitation 1876–8

Gladstone's moralistic approach to foreign affairs developed most clearly in opposition to the Conservative government in the second half of the 1870s. In assuming the leadership of the **Bulgarian agitation** in 1876, Gladstone set himself against the mainstream trend of British government policy in the nineteenth century. This policy was to support the **Ottoman Empire** as a barrier against Russian expansion in the Near East (Middle East).

Bulgarian agitation: a movement of popular protest in Britain against the massacres of Bulgarian Christians carried out by the Turkish authorities in Bulgaria.

Ottoman Empire: the Turkish Empire, which in the 1870s included tracts of southeast Europe as well as land in Asia. The desire of groups such as the Bulgarians for national independence weakened the Empire. This helped to give rise to the 'Eastern Question', a long-running issue in nineteenth-century great power diplomacy.

The first major study of the episode was Richard Shannon's *Gladstone and the Bulgarian Agitation 1876* (1963). Shannon saw Gladstone's involvement in the anti-Turkish crusade mainly as a political manoeuvre, intended to establish his hold over the Liberal Party and its supporters. A different interpretation was provided by the American historian Ann Saab, who studied Gladstone's views on the region over a longer period in *Reluctant Icon: Gladstone, Bulgaria and the working classes, 1856–1878* (1991). Saab emphasised Gladstone's sincerity, arguing that he saw Bulgaria primarily as a moral issue. He was influenced partly by popular pressure within Britain and partly by a troubled conscience over his past support for the Crimean War, in which Britain and France had supported Turkey against Russia.

The trend of recent studies by historians, influenced by the publication of the Liberal leader's diaries, has been to emphasise the importance of his religious beliefs. It has also highlighted the underlying conservatism of many of his attitudes. In many ways Gladstone remained a supporter of Peel and of Peel's senior spokesperson on foreign affairs, Lord Aberdeen. Aberdeen had appointed Gladstone as Chancellor of the Exchequer in his government from 1852 to 1885. Peel and Aberdeen were representatives of an older Conservatism, which was less 'patriotic' and less aggressive compared to Disraeli's approach as Prime Minister.

The editor of the Gladstone diaries, H.C.G. Matthew, drew attention to the fact that, in spite of his verbal attacks on the Turks, the 'Grand Old Man' was not seeking independence for the territories under their rule. Instead, the legalistic side of his nature led him to support the idea that the Ottoman Empire should have suzerainty over its European subjects. Gladstone was critical of the Disraeli government because it had failed to support united action by the great powers, in order to compel the Turks to observe civilised standards of behaviour. His concern was with the moral conduct of rulers rather than with the political rights of the governed.

The historian Eugenio Biagini, in his book *Gladstone* (2000), supports Matthew's view by stressing Gladstone's conservative approach to foreign affairs. He argues that Gladstone's main concern was with the maintenance of European order. This was to be achieved by means of consultation between the Great Powers, in support of international treaties. His belief in the idea of national self-determination did not apply indiscriminately, but was limited to Christian nations and to those non-Christian nations that possessed stable governments.

The Midlothian Campaigns 1879–80

One of the most important ways Gladstone made known his views on foreign policy was in the Midlothian Campaigns. Having retired as leader of the Liberal Party in 1875, Gladstone campaigned for a parliamentary seat in the area around Edinburgh known as the county of Midlothian. During the campaign Gladstone developed his attack on the foreign and imperial policy of Disraeli's Conservative government of 1874–1880. He focused heavily on the government's involvement in the recent Afghan War and the Zulu War. The early stages of these wars involved disastrous defeats for

British forces. One of Gladstone's themes was the immorality of engaging in aggressive wars. 'Remember', he declared, 'that the sanctity of life in the hill villages of Afghanistan … is as **inviolable** in the eye of Almighty God as can be your own.' In the course of the campaigns he put forward six 'right principles of foreign policy':

Inviolable: sacred; unable to be broken without serious consequences.

- good government at home to conserve the strength of the Empire
- the preservation of peace
- the maintenance of the Concert of Europe
- avoidance of 'needless and entangling engagements'
- the equal rights of all nations
- a love of freedom.

As Biagini points out in his analysis of the Midlothian Campaigns, Gladstone attacked both the immoral nature of war and its financial costs. He was particularly concerned that Disraeli's government had broken the principles of sound finance by increasing military expenditure, which it funded by borrowing rather than increasing taxes.

Historians have often noted how difficult it was to turn the Midlothian ideals into practice after Gladstone returned to office in 1880. W.N. Medlicott's 1956 study, *Bismarck, Gladstone and the Concert of Europe,* showed how the belief in power politics that underpinned **Bismarck's alliance system** took precedence over Gladstone's vision of international co-operation. Soon after coming to power in 1880, Gladstone succeeded in organising a joint naval expedition by the Great Powers in the Adriatic Sea, in order to force the Turks to honour commitments to transfer land to Montenegro and Greece following the Treaty of Berlin. This was a short-lived success for the idea of a Concert of Europe. Bismarck had no interest in using German resources to support an abstract concept. He believed that countries should pursue their own interests, declaring that 'he who speaks of Europe is wrong. It is simply a geographical expression'.

Bismarck's alliance system: Bismarck concluded agreements with other powers in order to safeguard Germany's international position. This involved keeping France isolated, and maintaining links with both Austria and Russia.

Gladstone: out of his time or a victim of circumstances?

It would seem that Gladstone's views on foreign relations were simply out of place in an increasingly harsh international environment. However, on more than one occasion he found himself driven into authorising unilateral military action that left Britain isolated. The invasion of Egypt in 1882 created mistrust between Britain and France. Relations with Russia were damaged in the spring of 1885 when Gladstone responded to the Penjdeh incident by making preparations for possible military action.

As a consequence, a number of historians have held that the record of the 1880–55 government shows the lack of realism of the Midlothian principles. In his study *Splendid isolation?* (1999), for example, John Charmley writes that Gladstone was 'neither the first nor the last Liberal to discover that an ethical foreign policy is easier to preach than to practise'. In *The Mid-Victorian Generation 1846–1886*, K.T. Hoppen argues that Gladstone underestimated the very real differences between the European powers, mistakenly believing that a natural balance could be maintained in international affairs. A more favourable view is to be found in Eugenio Biagini's study *Gladstone*, yet even he concedes that his subject was the victim of hostile external circumstances. It seems unlikely that further research will alter this generally negative assessment of the foreign policy of Gladstone's second government.

Q Was Gladstone a reluctant imperialist?

1. Read the following extract and answer the question.

   'It made sense to treat the colonies with sensitivity for two good reasons: one, it would avoid another war of American independence, which Gladstone saw as quite needless; two, having acquired the Empire, it was clearly to be well governed. But it was not to be extended: he could conclude a long speech at Leeds in 1881 with the apparently contradictory statement – "And so, gentlemen, I say that while we are opposed to imperialism, we are devoted to the Empire".'

   (D.M. Schreuder, *Gladstone and Kruger: Liberal government and colonial 'home rule' 1880–85*, Routledge, 1969, p47.)

   ['*... war of American independence ...*' refers to the conflict between Britain and the North American colonies, which lasted from 1775 to 1783 and resulted in the establishment of the United States of America.]

   Using your own knowledge, how adequately does the extract above describe Gladstone's approach to the British Empire in the years 1868 to 1886?

2. To what extent was Gladstone forced into increasing the size of the British Empire during his Second Ministry, 1880–5?

Did Gladstone have 'a mission to pacify Ireland'?

Was he just responding to events?

What eventually made him convert to Irish Home Rule?

Was he consistent in his views?

Framework of events

1869	Gladstone passes Irish Church Disestablishment
1870	Irish Land Act
1873	Defeat of Irish Universities Bill
1877	Gladstone visits Ireland
1879	Foundation of the Land League
1880	Charles Stewart Parnell becomes leader of the Irish Nationalist Party
1881	Irish Land Act; arrest of Parnell
1882	Parnell released from jail; Phoenix Park murders
1885	Parnell forms alliance with Conservatives and campaigns against Liberals in November General Election; in December it becomes known that Gladstone is contemplating Irish Home Rule
1886	Gladstone takes office in February with Parnell's support; introduces Home Rule Bill, which splits the Liberal Party and is defeated in the House of Commons in June. Gladstone loses General Election in July
1890	Parnell ruined by involvement in divorce scandal
1893	Gladstone's second Home Rule Bill passes the Commons but is defeated in the Lords

THE quotation in the title of this section recalls one of the best-known incidents in nineteenth century British politics. Whilst awaiting Queen Victoria's summons to form his first government, in December 1868, Gladstone is said to have uttered the words, 'My mission is to pacify Ireland'. Historians sympathetic to Gladstone and Liberalism tended to interpret the events of the subsequent two and a half decades in the light of this statement. To them it started a period of consistent effort, on Gladstone's part, to solve the **Irish question** (see below) in a spirit of justice and fairness. Among the earliest of these writers was John Morley, author of the official life of Gladstone (1903), who was also a close friend and colleague of the Liberal leader in his last two Cabinets. The fact that Morley twice held the post of Chief Secretary for Ireland, and shared Gladstone's post-1886 enthusiasm for Irish Home Rule, certainly affected his interpretation of events.

This tradition was most fully expressed in the work of J.L. Hammond, whose thoroughly researched *Gladstone and the Irish Nation* appeared in 1938. Although Hammond acknowledged

The Irish question

The Irish question is a shorthand term for the complex of religious, social and political issues which affected relations between Britain and Ireland in the nineteenth century.

Religion

Although the majority of Irish people were Catholic, the Protestant minority – which was strongest in the north of Ireland (Ulster) – enjoyed considerable privilege and power. Ulster Protestants were determined to maintain their membership of the United Kingdom and to resist the demands of Irish Nationalists.

Socio-economic issues

There was a significant social and economic divide between the mainly rural south and the rapidly industrialising north. Although conditions varied according to locality, there was a conflict between poorer tenant farmers and the Anglo-Irish landlords who dominated the rural areas. (The Anglo-Irish were descendants of British settlers who established themselves as landowners in Ireland from the seventeenth century onwards.)

What was Home Rule?

Irish Home Rule aimed to give all of Ireland a form of internal self-government, but within the United Kingdom. Ireland would have its own elected parliament and government, just as Scotland does now. It was a form of devolution.

British governments were traditionally hostile to demands for Home Rule, fearing that it might endanger national security and the Empire.

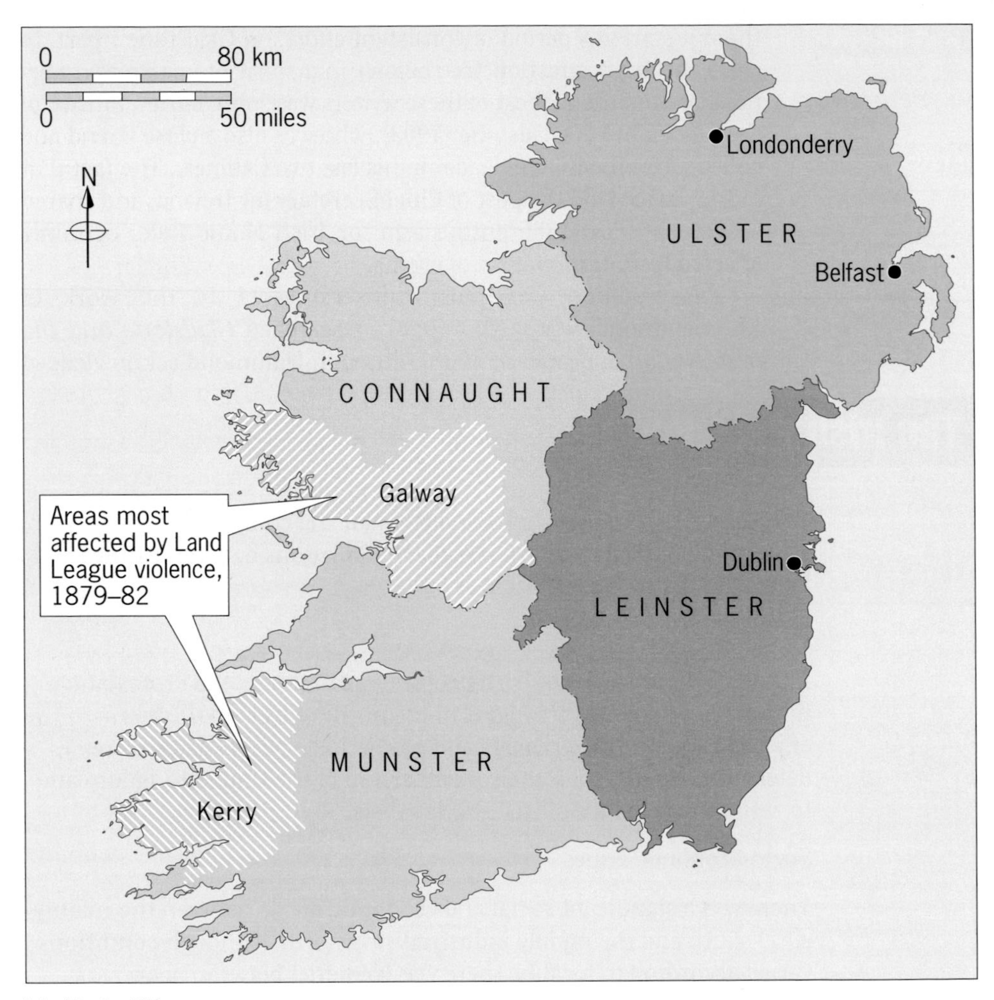

Ireland in the 1880s, showing its four provinces and two of its 32 counties, Galway and Kerry.

that Gladstone had been only intermittently interested in Ireland prior to 1868, after that date he saw Ireland's problems as a challenge to his moral sense. He hoped at first, by dealing with religious, social and economic issues, to satisfy the demands of the Irish people without conceding full self-government. Yet, according to Hammond, Gladstone was unique amongst British politicians in his sensitivity to the national character of the Irish people: 'from first to last he thought of the Irish as a people'; and again, 'he longed to see the Irish problem solved by a plan that gave Ireland her self-respect and England security'. Gladstone was motivated throughout by support for Liberal principles of freedom. Although events in Ireland sometimes compelled him to adopt a tough law-and-order policy (for example after the **Phoenix Park murders** in 1882), he was always reluctant to take this kind of action.

Phoenix Park murders: the murder in Dublin of the newly appointed Chief Secretary for Ireland, Lord Frederick Cavendish, and the senior civil servant in the administration, T.H. Burke, in May 1882. Although responsibility lay with a fringe extremist group, the Invincibles, the incident was a setback for the recently established links between Gladstone and Parnell.

In modified form the Morley/Hammond interpretation was an important influence on the next generation of historians. Foremost among them was F.S.L. Lyons, whose *Ireland since the Famine* (1971) became a standard textbook. He stressed the importance of Gladstone's own conscience and his awareness of the impact that the Irish problem had upon Britain's moral standing in Europe. Gladstone's wish to bring reform to Ireland came as a response to the **Fenian movement** in 1867. Gladstone interpreted violence as a sign of genuine Irish grievances and, in Lyons' words, now tried to 'woo Ireland from the paths of desperation by a sustained attempt at constructive reform'. The disestablishment of the Irish Church was Gladstone's first major reform on taking office. He introduced the reform because he knew it would be popular with both Irish Catholics and British Nonconformists. It was, however, primarily a matter of principle; Gladstone had for long been persuaded that it was unjust to support the Anglican Church (Church of Ireland) as the official religion, in a country where 80 per cent of the population was Catholic and 10 per cent was Nonconformist. Lyons argued that, for Gladstone, disestablishment was a necessary but not a sufficient answer to the Irish problem. His **1870 Irish Land Act** and his **1873 Irish Universities Bill** were the other parts of a programme intended to bring peace to Ireland.

Fenian movement: an Irish republican movement, founded in 1858 in the USA. It aimed to win independence from Britain using violence. In September 1867 a policeman was killed during an attempt to rescue Fenian prisoners in Manchester, and three months later there was a bomb explosion at Clerkenwell prison in London.

Irish Land Act (1870): an attempt to give legal protection to Irish tenant farmers. It extended to other parts of Ireland a custom which existed in Ulster, whereby tenants were able to claim compensation from landlords for improvements that the tenants made to their land holdings. It also included a limited attempt to help tenants purchase their farms. The Act failed to address the problems of tenants who were evicted because they could not pay their rent in times of economic hardship.

Irish Universities Bill (1873): an attempt by Gladstone's first government to create a university that would be neutral in religious terms, which Irish Catholics would feel able to attend. The bill failed to satisfy the Catholic Church, whilst also arousing the hostility of many Liberals, who felt that too many concessions to Catholic sensitivities had been made.

Was Gladstone just responding to events?

Sceptical: doubting generally accepted interpretations.

A more **sceptical** approach to Gladstone's policies surfaced in the writings of the historian John Vincent. In an important article published in *Proceedings of the British Academy* in 1977, he portrayed Gladstone as reluctantly responding to events, rather than introducing reforms. Vincent argued that Gladstone had little personal regard for the Irish people. Apart from briefly landing there during a cruise in 1880, he paid only one visit to Ireland. This was in 1877, and it was far from a comprehensive fact-finding tour. Vincent also questioned the idea that Gladstone took office in 1868 with a deeply felt 'mission' towards Ireland. According to Vincent, he took up the Irish Church question because his senior colleague, Lord Russell, had already raised it, and because he wanted to deprive the Conservatives of the opportunity to deal with the issue. It was also a convenient way of uniting the diverse elements in the Liberal Party. It also took attention away from the potentially divisive issues such as education and the secret ballot. In opposition once again after 1874, Gladstone's interest in Ireland declined. He remained convinced that his 1870 Land Act was an adequate solution to the problems of the tenant farmers, until forced in 1880–1 to modify his position. The agitation of the **Land League**, which compelled him to take action in the form of the **1881 Irish Land Act**, took him by surprise.

Land League: an organisation formed to protect Irish tenant farmers against the threat of eviction by landlords during the agricultural depression, which began in the mid-1870s. Its tactics included violence against landlords and their property.

Irish Land Act (1881): an attempt to address the shortcomings of the 1870 Land Act. It conceded the 'three Fs': Fair rent, to be fixed by a land court, in the event of a dispute between landlord and tenant; Free sale of a tenant's interest in his holding, when he moved to a new farm; and Fixity of tenure, (security of occupation) for tenants who met certain conditions.

With regard to the land issue, a similar view appeared in the work of the historian Allen Warren. His article, 'Gladstone, land and social reconstruction in Ireland 1881–1887' (*Parliamentary History*

THE RIVALS.

This *Punch* cartoon suggests that Gladstone's efforts to pacify Ireland ('Hibernia') are threatened by the violent intentions of the Land League terrorists. August, 1881

1983), emphasised the Liberal leader's reluctance to go beyond the 1870 Act. Warren argued that Gladstone, a social conservative at heart, wished above all to safeguard the traditional relationship between landlords and tenants. He saw this as a healthy basis for an orderly society. He was extremely reluctant to support proposals for extensive land purchase, whereby the government would make available large sums of money to allow peasants to buy land from landlords. This would create a class of peasant owner-occupiers. Gladstone was slow to adopt more radical measures and, claims Warren, thought little about the problems of Ireland between the early 1870s and the period 1880–1.

Keeping the party together

No understanding of Gladstone would be complete without an awareness of the calculations which he had to make as a party leader. Gladstone himself, many years later, identified the Irish Church as one of a handful of issues which he called his 'striking gift'. This he defined as 'an insight into the facts of particular eras, and their relations one to another, which generates in the mind a conviction that the materials exist for forming a public opinion, and for directing it to a particular end'. It is easy to understand how such a statement could be read as indicating a talent for grasping the most politically advantageous moment for action. Irish disestablishment certainly enabled Gladstone to hold together a broad coalition of Liberal support. It pleased the radicals, who saw it as an assault on traditional privilege, and it encouraged Nonconformists to hope for similar measures in the other parts of the United Kingdom. The Whigs, who had long accepted that the privileged status of the Irish Church was hard to defend, saw disestablishment as a way of reducing Catholic grievances against British rule. Michael Bentley, whose work shares the **'high political'** outlook of John Vincent, writes in *Politics without Democracy 1815–1914* (1984) that Gladstone's mission 'was to pacify the Liberal Party'. Similarly Roy Foster, author of another revisionist work, *Modern Ireland 1600–1972* (1988), depicted Gladstone as moving through 'a series of energetic but short-term reactions to immediate political problems.'

'High political': relating to the actions and calculations of leading politicians. This approach to political history assumes that the behaviour of politicians is governed largely by individual self-interest and not by ideological or moral issues.

Not all historians have accepted this emphasis on party management as the driving force behind Gladstone's Irish policies. After all, Ireland constituted a major administrative problem, which no mid-Victorian government could afford to ignore. In his commentary on the Gladstone diaries, H.C.G. Matthew acknowledged the usefulness of the Irish Church issue in uniting the Liberal Party, but also argued that it was part of a broader strategy to bring stability to Ireland. Gladstone's purpose was to get the Irish to accept union with the rest of the United Kingdom. This would be shown by demonstrating that the Westminster Parliament could deal with their concerns. According to Matthew, the 1870 Land Act and the Irish Universities Bill had a similarly conservative intention. By bringing forward these measures the government sought to demonstrate, in Gladstone's words, that 'there is nothing that Ireland has asked and which this country and this Parliament have refused'. Yet these policies failed to stop the growth of popular support for the Irish Home Rule Party. In the 1874 General Election 59 Home Rule MPs were returned. In 1880 the number rose to 63. As a result, Gladstone had to reassess his approach. If generous actions by the Westminster Parliament had failed to satisfy the Irish, the implication was that some form of self-government would have to be considered.

What eventually made Gladstone convert to Irish Home Rule?

Gladstone's decision to support Irish Home Rule, which became public knowledge in the winter of 1885–86, was perhaps the most controversial move of his entire career. His proposal to grant Ireland its own parliament split the Liberal Party. It caused almost a quarter of his MPs (94), and many of the party's supporters beyond Westminster, to reject his leadership. Their subsequent co-operation with the Conservatives brought about Gladstone's electoral defeat in the summer of 1886, and ensured that the Liberal Party would remain out of office for the greater part of the next 20 years. Gladstone's support for Home Rule also brought an end to the **Irish Nationalist Party's** attempt to hold the balance of power between the two British parties at Westminster. **Parnell** and his successors were now committed to a permanent alliance with the Liberals. It was now the only way of achieving their goal of a

Irish Nationalist Party: a political party formed in 1870 to campaign for the granting of Irish Home Rule – a parliament based in Dublin.

Charles Stewart Parnell (1846–91)
A Protestant landowner leading a mainly Catholic Nationalist Party, Parnell was dedicated to the achievement of Home Rule for Ireland. He transformed the party into a disciplined force in the House of Commons, using it from 1880–5 to disrupt parliamentary business and to draw attention to Irish issues. From 1886 Gladstone's support for Home Rule tied Parnell to an alliance with the Liberal Party. His career was wrecked in 1890 when a divorce case brought his long running affair with a married woman, Mrs Katharine O'Shea, to public attention.

self-governing Ireland. Why then did Gladstone take such a momentous step?

Political opportunism or the Christian solution?

To Gladstone's Conservative opponents at the time, it was a straightforward matter of political opportunism. The November 1885 General Election had resulted in a parliamentary deadlock, with 86 Irish Nationalists uneasily supporting a minority Conservative government. With 334 Liberal MPs facing 250 Conservatives, the stage was set for Gladstone to take office once again by winning over the Nationalists with promises of Home Rule. The leading Conservative, Lord Randolph Churchill, memorably portrayed Gladstone as 'an old man in a hurry', a political leader so desperate for high office that he would jeopardise the national interest and sacrifice the welfare of Ulster Protestants by forming an alliance with Irish nationalist rebels.

To those Liberals who remained loyal to Gladstone, the explanation was equally clear. The Grand Old Man (Gladstone), having tried over many years to bring justice and peace to Ireland, had finally concluded that only Home Rule would satisfy the country's legitimate demands for fair treatment. This view is supported by historians sympathetic to the Liberal tradition, such as J.L. Hammond. He argued that although Gladstone had originally hoped to settle the Irish question without conceding Home Rule, 'he alone among public men held from the first that Great Britain could not resist that

Landmark Study The book that changed people's views

A.B. Cooke and John Vincent,
The Governing Passion: Cabinet government and party politics in Britain 1885–86
(Harvester, 1974)

Cooke and Vincent caused controversy by focusing exclusively on the activities of a handful of important political figures, whom they saw as engaging in a continuous competition for power and office. Unlike previous historians, they regarded the public pronouncements of politicians as a cover for their selfish ambitions. They viewed Westminster as a closed, inward-looking world, insulated from popular pressures and wider concerns about public policy. It was, they wrote, 'a highly specialised community, like the City or Whitehall, whose primary interest was inevitably its own very private institutional life'.

This perspective led the two authors to see Gladstone as motivated by narrow party considerations rather than by ideological or moral concerns. Whilst acknowledging that he was not only a politician but also a conscientious, scholarly Christian, they argued that this did not affect his political conduct: 'Gladstone moved rapidly from one world and atmosphere to another and perhaps incompatible one, forgetting for the time all the other contexts in which he operated.'

The Governing Passion was criticised by a number of historians for its deliberately narrow focus. Historians such as H.C.G. Matthew and Terry Jenkins argued that Gladstone had a much more sincere and long-term interest in Ireland. Cooke and Vincent's work remains important because, although it may well reflect a partial version of reality, it has prompted a major debate on the means by which politicians reach their decisions.

demand if it were seriously made by the great majority of the Irish people'. With a majority of Irish parliamentary seats in the hands of Parnell's party from the autumn of 1885, the need for Home Rule was clear. When he privately approached the Conservative leaders in December 1885, with a suggestion that they take up Home Rule themselves, he was not – as they suspected – cunningly seeking to lure them into a potentially divisive policy. It was rather that, from a practical point of view, he believed that his opponents had a better chance of settling the problem. The Conservatives' control of the House of Lords gave them an important advantage in Parliament over the passage of legislation. Undeterred by the Conservatives' refusal to co-operate, Gladstone then introduced his own **Home Rule Bill** (see below) in a spirit of selfless duty.

A similar interpretation is to be found in the work of F.S.L. Lyons. In *Ireland since the Famine* he dismissed the charge that Gladstone was thinking in terms of selfish party advantage. He arrived at the decision in favour of Home Rule, 'as he had arrived at others of the cataclysmic decisions of his lifetime, by asking himself what was the right, ultimately the Christian, solution'. According to Lyons, the growth of support for self-government, and the rise of an Irish party committed to parliamentary methods, constituted an unanswerable moral case as far as Gladstone was concerned.

The early 1970s saw the appearance of several studies which viewed Gladstone in a less idealistic light. In *Liberal Politics in the Age of Gladstone and Rosebery* (1972), D.A. Hamer portrayed the adoption of Home Rule as a means of binding together the different

Gladstone's Home Rule Bill, 1886

- It proposed to create an Irish legislature (law-making body), based in Dublin, with an executive responsible to it and with power to raise taxes.
- The Westminster Parliament was to continue to be responsible for issues which affected the United Kingdom as a whole, including matters involving the Crown, foreign policy, defence, customs and excise, trade and navigation, coinage, weights and measures.
- The British government would retain control of the police in a transitional period.
- No Irish MPs were to attend the Westminster Parliament, although Ireland would pay a contribution to the United Kingdom Treasury.

strands within the party. The most controversial, however, was *The Governing Passion* by A.B. Cooke and John Vincent (1974), a detailed examination of high politics in 1885–6 (see **Landmark study**, p55). They argued that Home Rule was a device by which Gladstone sought to reassert his control over his party in the face of challenges to his position from rivals such as Lord Hartington and Joseph Chamberlain. They depicted him as lacking in fixed principles, and uncertain until a relatively late stage whether to give priority to Home Rule or to the **Land Purchase Bill**, which was also introduced in the spring of 1886. Instead of seeing Gladstone's policies as 'leading naturally towards Home Rule', Cooke and Vincent argued that 'they can equally well be read as leading in quite a different direction: towards diminishing the independence and strength of Irish nationalism, so as to benefit the Liberal Party and his position in it'.

Land Purchase Bill (1886): a proposal to buy out Irish landlords on a large scale, using large quantities of public money, in order to create a class of small peasant farming owner-occupiers. Although originally presented as inseparable from the Home Rule Bill, Gladstone quietly shelved the Land Purchase Bill as its unpopularity became increasingly clear.

'In Suspense. Or How Long Will It Last?' The cartoonist Tom Merry, in *St Stephen's Review*, depicts Gladstone saved from political destruction only by the votes of the Irish Nationalists. Looking on are Liberal Unionists, including Lord Hartington, John Bright and Joseph Chamberlain (second, third and fourth from right).

Was Gladstone consistent in his views?

The interpretation to be found in *The Governing Passion* has by no means commanded universal acceptance among historians. Cooke and Vincent were criticised for ignoring wider aspects of the contemporary scene and for viewing Irish policy as little more than the tool of cynical, self-interested politicians. In his article on Gladstone's land policy, Allen Warren argued that the Liberal leader took a serious interest in local self-government from at least 1881. Gladstone came to believe that, if land purchase were to be made to work, it would necessitate the creation of representative local institutions. These would not only provide security for the repayment of government loans but also compel the Irish people to act in a responsible manner and help to preserve the cohesion of rural society. By devolving power to the forces represented by Parnell, Gladstone aimed to contain the growth of more extreme forms of nationalism.

A similar agenda was seen by the historian James Loughlin, author of *Gladstone, Home Rule and the Ulster Question* (1986). He argued that Gladstone was mistaken in his assessment of the situation. He underestimated the financial cost of his policies and failed to appreciate the depth of Ulster Protestant hostility to his proposals. Nevertheless Loughlin did not fundamentally question the sincerity of the Liberal leader's attempt to resolve the Irish problem. He suggested that Gladstone produced Home Rule and land purchase as part of a comprehensive settlement. This was designed to satisfy the Irish people's desire for self-government, to recreate social harmony and reintegrate the landlord class into Irish society. According to Loughlin, Gladstone was persuaded to take action by exaggerated reports of the state of Irish unrest, including claims by a senior civil servant, Sir Robert Hamilton, that Ireland was on the verge of revolution. Gladstone came to believe that a decisive breach with past policies was necessary, and that only Home Rule could avert a serious crisis.

An idea that matured in Gladstone's mind

The publication of the relevant sections of Gladstone's diaries tended to support the idea that Home Rule matured gradually in his mind, and was not seized upon to suit his political convenience. In his commentary on the diaries, H.C.G. Matthew argued that there was 'no single moment of decision' in favour of Home Rule. In the autumn of 1885 Gladstone undertook extensive reading of books on constitutional theory and Irish history. This helped to confirm a growing conviction that the decentralisation of power was the most effective way of reconciling the Irish to the British connection. The parallel here was with the granting of self-governing status to Canada, which had chosen to remain within the British Empire. Matthew regards Gladstone's championing of Home Rule as a continuation of his long-standing 'mission of pacification', in which the means changed but the underlying purpose remained the same.

The reaction against *The Governing Passion* has continued in the most recent work on the period. In his book *The Liberal Ascendancy 1830–1886* (1994), Terry Jenkins produced important evidence, notably a diary entry by Lord Derby from early October 1885, which indicated that Gladstone's mind had been moving towards Home Rule before the November 1885 General Election. The Liberal leader had to be cautious about making a public statement because he feared that it might open up divisions within the party. Jenkins focuses attention on the final month of the second Gladstone government as a turning point. In May-June 1885 the Cabinet was deeply divided over Joseph Chamberlain's proposals for a local self-government scheme for Ireland, the 'central board' scheme. Although the proposal fell short of the Irish Nationalist demand for a parliament, the ensuing controversy within the Liberal government persuaded Gladstone that he must continue as leader in order to resolve the problem.

Richard Shannon, whose biography *Gladstone: Heroic Minister 1865–1898* appeared in 1999, presented Gladstone as keeping an open mind on the subject of Home Rule for some years prior to 1885. As early as February 1882, he apparently invited a debate by publicly asking the Irish Nationalists whether it was possible to devise a scheme which reconciled local self-government with the supremacy of the Westminster Parliament. Shannon argues that Gladstone's thoughts on Home Rule crystallised in March 1885, following a speech by the Nationalist MP William O'Brien that made a great impression on him. Gladstone could not make public his support for Home Rule until much later, but by the late summer of 1885 he was fully determined to lead both his party and the country in that direction. The Home Rule episode, for Shannon, fits with his overall interpretation of Gladstone as an authoritarian party leader who manipulated public opinion. Once he had persuaded himself of a course of action, his practice was 'to generate in the public mind a conviction corresponding to his doings and intentions'.

An agreement now seems to be emerging among historians regarding Gladstone's support for Home Rule. The cynical thesis of *The Governing Passion,* that his actions should be interpreted purely in terms of short-term political tactics, has not proved convincing for most historians. As K.T. Hoppen argues in *The Mid-Victorian Generation 1846–1886,* few accept the idea that public pronouncements are merely a cover for political conspiracies. It seems clear that Gladstone had begun to move decisively towards Home Rule well before the 1885 General Election, and this outcome was not completely inconsistent with his earlier career. Although, as a practical politician, his position in Parliament was central to him, he did have a genuine desire to solve the problems of Ireland. Statesmanship, as much as politics, shaped Gladstone's response to the Irish question.

Q

Did Gladstone have 'a mission to pacify Ireland'?

1. Read the following extract and answer the question.

   'He did not want to encourage the demand for Home Rule. He hoped that it might be possible to satisfy Irish national sentiment with something short of a special Parliament. On the other hand, he alone among public men held from the first that Great Britain could not resist that demand if it were seriously made by the great majority of the Irish people.'

   (J.L. Hammond, *Gladstone and the Irish Nation*, Longman, 1938, p402.)

   Using this extract and your own knowledge, consider how far Gladstone was a genuine supporter of Home Rule for Ireland.

2. How justified is the view that Gladstone's attitude to the problems of Ireland was determined by party political considerations?

Gladstone: an assessment

Gladstone and the Liberal Party

Gladstone combined an intense religious and moral sense with great administrative drive and the skills of a calculating politician.

He held together a political party with a wide variety of differing views. He did this by focusing the Liberal Party on unifying issues, such as Irish Church disestablishment (1868), anti-imperialism (1879–80) and Irish Home Rule (1886 onwards).

Imperial and foreign affairs

Although not a pacifist, Gladstone favoured an overseas policy that maintained peace and restricted Britain's external commitments.

In practice, the preservation of British interests meant that there were important areas of similarity and continuity between Conservative and Liberal governments in this period.

The Irish question

Gladstone was not simply interested in pursuing justice for the Irish people but was aware of the impact of Irish matters on the Liberal Party.

His motives for supporting Home Rule after 1885 remain controversial. He seems to have been seeking political and social stability in Ireland as well as securing his position as Liberal Party leader against rivals such as Joseph Chamberlain.

Gladstone's legacy

Gladstone's campaign for Irish Home Rule divided his party from 1886 into two parts: the Gladstonian Liberals and the Liberal Unionists. In the period 1886 to 1905, the Liberal Party only managed to hold power from 1892 to 1895 thanks to the support of the Irish Home Rule Party.

In Gladstone's final years in national politics (1890–4) the Liberal Party moved in a more radical direction, although his own attitudes remained conservative on many issues. Gladstone resigned as Prime Minister in 1894 because he opposed increasing expenditure on the Royal Navy.

He had little sympathy with expanding the British Empire. He was also not enthusiastic about social reform. These both appeared to be popular political ideas in the late nineteenth century.

He remained an inspiration to his party even after he had retired. He had been a leading member of the Liberals from the 1850s. He had been Prime Minister and leader of the Liberals from 1868. Gladstone's support for free trade remained Liberal Party policy until the early 1930s. Support for free trade helped win a landslide victory for the Liberals in the January 1906 election.

Further reading

Texts specifically designed for students

Adelman, P. *Great Britain and the Irish Question 1800–1922* (Hodder and Stoughton, 1996)

Biagini, E.F. *Gladstone* (Palgrave/Macmillan, 2000)

Goodlad, G.D. *British Foreign and Imperial Policy 1865–1919* (Routledge, 2000)

Jenkins, T.A. *The Liberal Ascendancy 1830–1886* (Palgrave/Macmillan, 1994)

Texts for more advanced study

Cooke, A.B and Vincent, J. *The Governing Passion: Cabinet government and party politics in Britain 1885–86* (Harvester, 1974) is a highly controversial 'high political' interpretation of the Irish Home Rule crisis.

Hamer, D.A. *Liberal Politics in the Age of Gladstone and Rosebery* (Oxford University Press, 1972) argues that Gladstone used great political causes to control the Liberal Party.

Hammond, J.L. *Gladstone and the Irish Nation* (Longman, 1938) is the classic statement of the view that Gladstone had a sense of mission towards Ireland.

Matthew, H.C.G. *Gladstone 1809–1898* (Oxford University Press, 1997) contains the introductions to the full series of Gladstone diaries.

Parry, J.P. *The Rise and Fall of Liberal Government in Victorian Britain* (Yale University Press, 1993) sees Gladstone as representing an ultimately disastrous departure from the Whig tradition of political leadership.

Robinson, R. and Gallagher, J. *Africa and the Victorians: the official mind of imperialism* (Macmillan, 1961) began the modern debate on the reasons for Gladstone's intervention in Egypt.

Shannon, R. *Gladstone 1809–1865* (Hamish Hamilton, 1982) and *Gladstone 1865–1898: Heroic Minister* (Penguin, 1999) is the fullest modern biography.

Vincent, J. *The Formation of the British Liberal Party 1857–68* (Constable, 1966) broke new ground in its analysis of the composition of the party.

Index

Historians

Profiles

Main Index